The Anatomy of Racial Inequality

The W. E. B. Du Bois Lectures

The Anatomy of Racial Inequality

GLENN C. LOURY

HARVARD UNIVERSITY PRESS
Cambridge, Massachusetts, and London, England

Printed in the United States of America

First Harvard University Press paperback edition, 2003

Library of Congress Cataloging-in-Publication Data

Loury, Glenn C.
The anatomy of racial inequality / Glenn C. Loury
p. cm.—(W. E. B. Du Bois lectures)
Includes bibliographical references and index.
ISBN 0-674-00625-9 (cloth)
ISBN 0-674-01242-9 (paper)
1. African Americans—Social conditions—1975–
2. African Americans—Economic conditions.
3. African Americans—Civil rights.
4. Race discrimination—United States.
5. Race discrimination—Political aspects—United States.
6. United States—Race relations.
7. United States—Race relations—Political aspects.
I. Title II. Series.

E185.615 .L675 2001
305.896'073—dc21 2001039192

To Thomas C. Schelling—
mentor, colleague, and friend—
whose example I strive to emulate

CONTENTS

PREFACE

This book emerges from the W. E. B. Du Bois Lectures which I delivered at Harvard University in April 2000. I wish to thank Professor Henry Louis Gates Jr., Director of the Du Bois Institute for Afro-American Research at Harvard, and his colleagues, for the invitation to give those lectures.

However, this book has been gestating for many years. It grows out of my efforts over nearly three decades to understand the causes of black Americans' social and economic marginality, and to find possible remedies for this situation. The first chapter of my doctoral dissertation (submitted in 1976 to the Economics Department at the Massachusetts Institute of Technology, and written under the inspiring supervision of Prof. Robert M. Solow) was called "A Dynamic Theory of Racial Income Differences." Ideas from this early work underlie many of the arguments to be found in Chapters 3 and 4. More recently, in 1993, I collaborated with Stephen Coate of Cornell University on a paper entitled

"Will Affirmative Action Policies Eliminate Negative Stereotypes?" which appeared in the *American Economic Review*. Much of the analysis in Chapter 2 derives from this collaborative research.

Then, in 1997 (with the full support of my university's administration, for which I am grateful), I founded the Institute on Race and Social Division at Boston University (IRSD), in order to encourage the exchange of ideas on these themes among scholars working in the humanities and the social sciences. It has been both my privilege and a source of great pleasure to observe an outstanding interdisciplinary community of researchers coalesce around IRSD over these past four years. Exposure to these creative and learned colleagues has broadened and deepened my understanding of the subject and has contributed to my own thinking in ways too many and too subtle to enumerate. I should say, however, that my theory of "racial stigma" sketched in Chapter 3 and my critique offered in Chapter 4 of "race-blindness" as a moral ideal would never have come to fruition without the constant encouragement and periodic provocations of this extraordinary group of scholars.

I am also grateful to the many individuals who read and commented upon earlier drafts of this book. It has certainly benefited from their criticism—especially that of Henry Aaron, Marcellus Andrews, William Bowen, Samuel Bowles, Kerwin Charles, Jorge Garcia, Nathan Glazer, Mark Kleiman, Linda Datcher Loury, Jane Mansbridge, Deirdre McCloskey, Robert Nozick, Orlando Patterson, Steven Pinker, John Skrentny,

Steven Teles, Ajume Wingo, and Christopher Winship. I would also like to express my appreciation for the financial support of the work reflected here that has been provided by the Ford Foundation, the Andrew W. Mellon Foundation, the W. K. Kellogg Foundation, the John Templeton Foundation, and the Lynde and Harry Bradley Foundation.

Finally, I must acknowledge my intellectual indebtedness to a great economist, Thomas C. Schelling, to whom this book is dedicated. Shortly after arriving at Harvard in 1982 as a newly appointed Professor of Economics and of Afro-American Studies, I began to despair of the possibility that I could successfully integrate my love of economic science with my passion for thinking broadly and writing usefully about the issue of race in contemporary America. How, I wondered, could one do *rigorous* theoretical work in economics while remaining relevant to an issue that seemed so fraught with political, cultural, and psychological dimensions? Tom Schelling not only convinced me that this was possible; he took me by the hand and showed the way. The intellectual style reflected in this book developed under his tutelage. My first insights into the problem of "racial classification" emerged in lecture halls at Harvard's Kennedy School of Government, where, for several years in the 1980s, Tom and I co-taught a course we called "Public Policies in Divided Societies." Tom Schelling's creative and playful mind, his incredible breadth of interests, and his unparalleled mastery of strategic analysis opened up a new world of intellectual possibilities for me. I will always be grateful to him.

The Anatomy of Racial Inequality

1

INTRODUCTION

THIS BOOK is a meditation on the problem of racial inequality in the United States, focusing specifically on the case of African Americans. The argument to come will be abstract, theoretical, offering causal accounts and normative judgments. In making it I rely on, but am not confined by, my background in economics. I also draw on relevant scholarly literatures in sociology, political science, and history. Though no new evidence is presented, this treatment points to a novel conceptual framework for assimilating the evidence at hand. I will convey that framework with the aid of simple, stylized "models"—that is, thought experiments which illustrate the workings of hypothetical but plausible causal mechanisms. My goal with this exposition is to clarify how the phenomenon called "race"[1] operates so as to perpetuate the inter-group status disparities that are so readily observed in American social life.

One overriding reality motivates this reflection: Nearly a century and a half after the destruction of the institution of slavery, and a half-century past the dawn of the civil rights movement, social life in the United States continues to be characterized by significant racial stratification. Numerous indices of well-being—wages, unemployment rates, income and wealth levels, ability test scores, prison enrollment and crime victimization rates, health and mortality statistics—all reveal substantial racial disparities. Indeed, over the past quarter-century the disadvantage of blacks[2] along many of these dimensions has remained unchanged, or, in some instances, has even worsened. There has, of course, been noteworthy progress in reversing historical patterns of racial subordination. Still, there is no scientific basis upon which to rest the prediction that a rough parity of socioeconomic status for African Americans will be realized in the foreseeable future.[3] So we have a problem; it will be with us for a while; and it behooves us to think hard about what can and should be done.

THREE AXIOMS

As a starting point for the analysis I adopt three postulates, or axioms, about "race" and inequality in the United States. I use the term "axiom" here in the mathematical sense: an assumption embraced for the sake of argument, the implications of which may be of interest. I do not claim that these axioms are self-evident, merely that they are not implausible and are worthy of exploration. My goal in this book is to uncover the conclusions regarding "race" and social justice in the United States that are entailed by these assumptions.

> *Axiom 1 (Constructivism):* "Race" is a socially constructed mode of human categorization. That people use marks on the bodies of others to divide the field of human subjects into the subgroups we call "races" is a social convention for which no deeper justification in biological taxonomy is to be had.
>
> *Axiom 2 (Anti-Essentialism):* The enduring and pronounced social disadvantage of African Americans is not the result of any purportedly unequal innate human capacities of the "races." Rather, this disparity is a social artifact—a product of the peculiar history, culture, and political economy of American society.
>
> *Axiom 3 (Ingrained Racial Stigma):* An awareness of the racial "otherness" of blacks is embedded in the social consciousness of the American nation owing to the historical fact of slavery and its aftermath. This inherited stigma even today exerts an inhibiting effect on the extent to which African Americans can realize their full human potential.

I defend Axiom 1—the claim that "race" is best viewed in social, not biological terms—in the next chapter. The position on anti-essentialism in Axiom 2 has simply been assumed, not reached as a conclusion after a review of empirical evidence. There is, of course, an ongoing debate among social scientists about the sources, extent, and significance of racial differences in intelligence. In my opinion, the evidence emerging from this debate does not support the view that the social and economic disadvantage of blacks in America can be explained in terms of supposed innate differences in the intellectual abilities of the "races." But this book is not the place to make that case. In any event, I will in due course offer a deeper argument, to the effect that in a democratic polity devoted to civic equality the position on anti-essentialism taken here ultimately must be adopted as an a priori commitment, and not as a conclusion held tentatively or made contingent on the interpretation of evidence.

Concerning the assumption of "ingrained racial stigma," I provide a more extended justification in Chapter 3. For now, I wish merely to note that astute external observers of race relations in the United States have often stressed just this point. Thus in the early nineteenth century one finds Alexis de Tocqueville remarking that "the prejudice rejecting the Negroes seems to increase in proportion to their emancipation, and inequality cuts deep into mores as it is effaced from the laws" (Tocqueville 1848, 316). And at mid-twentieth century one finds Gunnar Myrdal pointing out the power of "vicious circles" of cumulative causation—self-sustaining processes in which the failure of blacks to make progress justified for whites the very prejudicial attitudes that, when reflected in social and political action, served to ensure that blacks would not advance (Myrdal 1944). I will suggest that subtle processes of this kind are at work among us, even today, and that a proper study of contemporary racial inequality requires one to identify such tragic, self-perpetuating processes, and in so doing, to lay bare the deeper, structural causes of African-American disadvantage.

Thus, the descriptive and the normative analyses to be offered here are closely connected. I endeavor to fathom the deeper causes of racial inequality so that, ultimately, I can assess the public morality of American social policy on this issue. So I will be addressing the question of "racial justice." Again, my approach is theoretical and conceptual. I make an effort to specify the criteria that ought to be consulted in such reflections. This leads me naturally into the fields of social and political philosophy, where such considerations have long been at the forefront. I end up questioning whether liberal political theory, the ruling orthodoxy on such matters, is adequate to this task of assessment. My concern is that liberal theory, as it has come to be practiced, gives insufficient weight to history—especially to the enduring and deeply rooted racial disparity in life chances characteristic of American society. One implication of liberal individualism especially important in current policy debate is the notion that public agents should be "colorblind"—that is, they should pay no heed to racial identities when formulating and executing policy. This view, I am convinced, is quite wrong, and I argue strenuously against it.

AN OVERVIEW

With these ambitions in view, the next three chapters successively address the topics Racial Stereotypes, Racial Stigma, and Racial Justice. Here is a brief overview of the argument.

The "stereotype" theme to which I will turn next deals with issues of information, incentives, and group reputation. Of the three topics, this is the one based most strictly in economics. My treatment takes as a point of departure collaborative research I published in the early 1990s with the economist Stephen Coate of Cornell University (Coate and Loury 1993a, 1993b). The key ideas can be conveyed without the burden of any technical apparatus and provide a valuable foundation for the subsequent analysis.

The main goal in Chapter 2 is to illustrate the sense in which it can be "rational" for an observer to use racial information to assess a subject's functionally relevant but nonracial traits, assuming that those traits are not directly observable. For instance, an employer concerned about a worker's productivity, a lender worried about a borrower's risk of default, or a policeman wanting to arrest a criminal may find that, on the average, their objectives are better served when they deal on different terms with the persons whom they perceive as belonging to different "races," and this despite the fact that "race" has no objective association with the underlying productivity, creditworthiness, or law-abidingness of individuals in society. Yet, this appearance of rationality notwithstanding, I go on to show how such racially stereotypic reasoning can in fact reflect modes of social cognition subtly biased against blacks, and I suggest that this kind of bias can serve to perpetuate and legitimate profound racial inequities.

These observations point in a natural way toward the topic of Chapter 3—"racial stigma," a sociological notion at some remove from my discipline of economics. Nevertheless, as will soon become clear, the concept of racial stigma is central to my thinking. My approach is loosely modeled on the work of the sociologist Erving Goffman.[4] Goffman's key concept is the notion of "virtual social identity" (Goffman 1963). This is the identity unreflectively imputed to someone by observers who, not being privy to extensive idiosyncratic information, draw conclusions about a person's deeper qualities on the basis of the easily observable indicators that may lie at hand. This imputed identity is "virtual" because it can diverge from the subject's actual identity; and it is "social" because the imputation occurs within the context of the social encounter and is structured by the nature of the social relationship that obtains between the subject and the observer.

One can immediately see a connection between this "stigma" notion and the concept of "stereotype" just mentioned. Both entail management by human agents of social situations where information about the people being encountered is limited. Yet the discussion in Chapter 3 makes clear that subtle and important distinctions can be drawn between these two notions. In particular, I will suggest that while "stigma" involves stereotyping it is, for the study of the problem of racial inequality, the more profound idea. Indeed, I will argue that "racial stigma" should now be given pride of place over "racial discrimination" as the concept which best reflects the causes of African-American disadvantage.

Chapter 4 is devoted to a discussion of racial justice. I wish to dispel at the outset any misconception that, because I am willing to use the words "race" and "justice" in the same sentence, I must of necessity be engaged in a rear-guard defense of affirmative action (though such a defense can be mounted and I am not at all reluctant to do so). That is not my primary purpose here. I am after bigger fish.

Nothing, in my opinion, reveals the intellectual shallowness of the discourse on racial inequality in contemporary American society more clearly than does this tendency, found among academics and journalists alike, to equate a critical analysis of "race" and social equity with the advocacy of racial preferences. One need only visit a courthouse, public hospital emergency room, or welfare office in any large American city to find compelling evidence that now, some seven score years after the end of slavery, American society is still marred by the social disadvantage of African Americans. When this fact is decried, increasingly one encounters this retort: "Why should a concern about social deprivation take any notice of 'race,' if no person is being victimized by racial discrimination?"

Of course, that "if" is a big one! But let us for the sake of argument set that point to one side for the moment. The commonplace claim that discrimination must be proven as the cause of inequality for questions of racial justice to arise is, from the perspective that I am developing here, both wrong and dangerous. My argument in Chapter 4 is aimed directly at refuting this claim.

WHY FOCUS ON BLACKS?

Some readers will object to a discussion of "racial inequality" that focuses on blacks, in light of the presence in American society of other nonwhites whose condition is aptly described as "disadvantaged." My view is that the case of African Americans is sufficiently distinctive—politically, historically, and sociologically—to warrant the focused analysis offered here. It is undeniable that articulations of and reactions to the claims of blacks are now driving forces in American politics, and this has been the case for many decades. While it is certainly true that Americans of varied backgrounds have over the course of the nation's history encountered, and in some cases continue to suffer, mistreatment because of their "race," the duration and severity of discrimination against the African slaves and their descendants have been unprecedented in American history. Only Native Americans have had an experience that could plausibly be seen as comparable, and that is a subject obviously requiring its own treatment.

Also, while status attainment of Americans from many backgrounds has been impeded by customs, practices, attitudes, beliefs, prejudices, and stereotypes, some reflecting perception and treatment by outsiders but some internal to the groups, African Americans are virtually unique in that any such attitudes, prejudices, and customs—particularly those inhibiting achievement that are internal to the group—have evolved almost entirely under the influence of, and often in reaction to, racially oppressive economic and political institutions indigenous to U.S. society. This is less true of the other nonwhite American ethnic groups whose numbers have swelled in recent decades owing to a large influx of immigrants from Asia and Latin America.

This is not a trivial point. Some conservative writers attribute black American disadvantage entirely or in part to purported patterns of "social pathology" said to be characteristic of "black culture."[5] Yet even were that to be so—and the point is eminently arguable—such "pathology" could not be rightly understood as an alien cultural blemish imposed on an otherwise pristine Euro-American canvas. Rather, it could only be seen as a domestic product, made over the generations wholly in the good old USA, for which the entire nation bears a responsibility. Clearly, this would not be the case—at least, not to the same degree—were there to be found any comparable, adverse cultural patterns among (say) Dominican or Korean immigrants.

In light of such political, historical, and sociological considerations, I conclude that the severe and protracted disadvantage of blacks, whatever its causes, is a profoundly troubling problem for American society, one that is distinct from and ethically more disturbing than would be the challenge posed by a comparable disparity in the social position of other nonwhite ethnic groups.[6] In reaching this conclusion, I do not imply that social disadvantage among nonblack racial minorities is of little scholarly or political interest. To the contrary, though it is motivated by the African-American experience, I believe this analysis offers insights that will prove useful for the broader study of racial inequality in the United States. Indeed, while I advance these reflections in the specific context of American society, and while I focus on the economic, political, social, and historical experience of blacks, I nevertheless hope to contribute with the theoretical development that follows to a deeper understanding of the problem of "race" and social marginality as it manifests itself in a great many societies around the globe. And now, on to the argument!

2

RACIAL STEREOTYPES

I RELY HEAVILY in this book on the elementary observation that, in the first instance, "race" is a mode of perceptual categorization people use to navigate their way through a murky, uncertain social world. I want us to think about people as being hungry for information, constantly seeking to better understand the social environment in which they are embedded, searching always for markers, guideposts, clues that can equip them to make wiser choices on matters of consequence. This is a *cognitive*, not a *normative* activity. Information-hungry human agents—in making pragmatic judgments, to be sure, but also as a necessity for survival—will notice visible, physical traits presented by those whom they encounter in society: their skin color, hair texture, facial bone structure, and so forth. There is neither shame nor mystery in this. The practice of grouping people together on the basis of their common possession of visible bodily marks is a universal aspect of the human condition.[1] One of the ways that we generate and store social information is to classify the persons we encounter—that is, form broad categories between which contrasts can be drawn and about which generalizations can be made—so we can better know what is to be expected from those with whom we must deal, but about whom all too little can be discerned. So I would like to begin with a few observations about the act of "racial classification."[2]

RACIAL CLASSIFICATION AS A COGNITIVE ACT

As befits an economist, I employ the concept of classification in the decision-theoretic sense: Decision-makers (*agents*) act in ways that affect others (*subjects*) on the basis of what can be observed about those toward whom their actions are directed. An employer hires, a banker lends, a landlord rents, a neighbor moves, a suitor woos, or not, and so on. As a purely cognitive matter, agents, surveying the field of human subjects, endeavor to discern relevant distinctions among subjects in that field in order to refine their actions, that those actions may better serve their ends. To make a distinction of this kind is to engage in an act of "classification" in the sense that I intend here. When distinctions are based in some way on a subject's "race," then we are dealing with an act of "racial classification."

Two things should be obvious straightaway: First, whether "race" is a part of the calculation or not, classifying human subjects in this general way is a universal practice, one that lies at the root of all social-cognitive behavior. There can only be the question of how, not whether, human agents will classify those subject to their actions. Second, at this level of generality, the normative status of even a race-based classification cannot be definitively assessed absent some consideration of the purposes on behalf of which the classifying act has been undertaken. That is, the simple fact that a person classifies others (or herself, for that matter) in terms of "race" is in itself neither a good nor a bad thing. Normative judgment must, at the very least, entail some analysis of the goals of classifying agents.

I stress this last point because it has apparently eluded some commentators on race relations in American life who argue that, since no exact biological taxonomy can vindicate the "race" idea, any use of this category for classificatory purposes is, *ipso facto,* morally dubious. But that cannot be correct. Even the current U.S. Supreme Court, in its doctrine of "strict scrutiny," recognizes that whether or not the reasons for a racial classification are *compelling* should constitute one of the tests to determine if it passes muster in constitutional terms. Yet the point is much more general. For both the racist employer (bent on holding blacks down) and the diligent public servant (intent on enforcing the laws against discrimination) will alike and necessarily be "guilty" of classifying the field of human subjects in racial terms as they carry forward their respective, diametrically opposed projects.[3] It follows that the cognitive act of so classifying is insufficient, by itself, to allow a normative judgment.

By focusing on racial classification I pose the question in a manner that may be contrasted with the more traditional focus on racial discrimination. In doing so I do not imply that no problems of racism or race-based unfairness in U.S. society still exist. To the contrary, although the extent of overt racial discrimination against blacks has obviously declined over the last half-century, it seems to me equally obvious that racial injustice in U.S. social, economic, and political life persists, though less transparently so, and in ways that are more difficult to root out. So, at any rate, I will be arguing here. I give pride of place to classification over discrimination for two reasons—generality and utility: Classification is the logically prior concept; and thinking in terms of classification yields greater insight into the problem at hand than thinking in terms of discrimination. The first point is a trivial one, once we see that discerning a difference is a necessary condition for acting on one. That my approach is more useful will, I trust, be clear when the reader has finished this book.

WHAT IS RACE?

I want now to say more formally what I intend by the term "race." In this book I use that term to refer to *a cluster of inheritable bodily markings carried by a largely endogamous group of individuals, markings that can be observed by others with ease, that can be changed or misrepresented only with great difficulty, and that have come to be invested in a particular society at a given historical moment with social meaning.* This definition has three aspects: ease of identification, relative immutability, and social signification. While physical markings on the human body are central to my notion of "race," I stress (in keeping with Axiom 1) that nothing turns on the underlying biological factors that may engender those markings. I only require that the pertinent physical traits are passed on across generations, are easily discerned, and are not readily disguised. Moreover, *what is "essential" here is that these physical traits are taken to signify something of import within an historical context.* "Race," on my account, is all about embodied social signification. As such, much depends on the processes through which powerful meanings come to be associated with particular bodily marks. Obviously, these will have to be historically specific, culturally mediated processes.[4]

There has been much recent discussion in philosophy and cultural studies about the ontological status of "race"—are there any things in the world that may be taken as corresponding to the word "race," and so forth. It has become fashionable to put the word in quotes, by way of emphasizing its problematic scientific and philosophical status. The core claim in this literature is that there exist no objective criteria—biological, cultural, or genealogical—through use of which the set of human beings can be consistently partitioned into a relatively small number of mutually exclusive, collectively exhaustive subsets that may be taken as races. Belief in the existence of races, on this view, is rather like belief in the existence of witches—just mischievous superstition, nothing more.[5] I do not follow this line of argument here.

Of course, neither do I dispute the core claim—Axioms 1 and 2 declare as much. But I find little of interest in this philosophy of language exercise. Rather, I am impressed, as any good social scientist would be, by the fact that so much human behavior has become organized around racial categorization, despite its evident lack of any basis in biological taxonomy. *This,* it would appear, is what must be explained. One has no need for *objective* rules of racial taxonomy to study, as I do here, the *subjective* use of racial classifications. It is enough that influential observers (passersby on the street, new neighbors before the moving van arrives, policemen, employers, bankers, and so on) hold schemes of classification in their minds, and act on those schemes. They need not make their schemes explicit; their methods of classification may well be mutually inconsistent, one with another. And while it may be true that these agents could not give cogent reasons for adopting their schemes, it is also the case that they are unlikely ever to be asked to do so.

Still, if a person is aware that others in society are inclined to classify him on the basis of certain markers and if, in turn, this classification constitutes the basis of differential actions affecting his welfare, then these markers will become important to him. He will attend to them, become conscious (and, I dare say, self-conscious) in regard to them. He will, at some level, understand and identify himself as being "raced."[6] This will be a rational cognitive stance on his part, not a belief in magic, and certainly not a *moral* error.[7]

Moreover, whatever the *scientific* status of the race concept, the *social convention* of classifying people on the basis of their bodily markings will typically have profound, enduring, and all too real consequences. This ubiquitous practice can, at one and the same time, be eminently consistent with reason, stubbornly resistant to change, and a formidable barrier to the attainment of social justice. To illustrate how and why this can be so, I want now to consider in some detail the inner workings of what I will call "self-confirming racial stereotypes."

SELF-CONFIRMING RACIAL STEREOTYPES

A "self-confirming stereotype" is a statistical generalization about some class of persons regarding what is taken *with reason* to be true about them as a class, but cannot be readily determined as true or false for a given member of the class. Furthermore, this generalization is "reasonable" in the specific sense that it is *self-confirming:* Observers, by acting on the generalization, set in motion a sequence of events that has the effect of reinforcing their initial judgment. And so a "self-confirming racial stereotype" is simply a generalization of this kind about a class of persons defined in part or altogether on the basis of whatever categories of racial classification happen to be operative in observers' minds. I wish to consider the rationality, durability, efficiency, and fairness of self-confirming racial stereotypes.

Obviously, a generalization about some group can be supported by evidence without that evidence having in any way been influenced by the actions of those making the generalization. Thus not all "reasonable" stereotypes will be self-confirming. However, I am interested here in the special circumstance in which those making a surmise about some group of persons have within their power the ability to act so as to influence the population being observed. For reasons that will become clear, I see this particular circumstance as being highly relevant to the task of understanding and evaluating the social problem of persistent racial inequality in the United States.

I acknowledge that this use of the term "stereotype" diverges from common parlance. *Webster's New World Dictionary* defines "stereotype" as "A fixed idea or popular conception about how a certain type of person looks, acts, etc." One senses a connotation of "unreasonableness" in that definition—the stereotype being a false or too simplistic surmise about some group: "blacks are lazy," "Jews are cunning," and so on. While I do not dispute that this crude overgeneralizing behavior occurs, it is not my subject here. Rather, my model of stereotypes is designed to show the limited sense in which even "reasonable" generalizations, those for which ample supporting evidence can be found, are fully "rational." I argue that such generalizations often represent instances of what I will refer to as "biased social cognition."

The self-confirming property of stereotypes as defined here is, therefore, crucial to my argument. I will be positing situations in which stereotypic thinking seems plausible, so I can go on to show that, even then, where race is involved things may not be quite as they appear.

To illustrate, if agents hold a negative stereotype about blacks they may think (correctly) that, on the average and all else equal, commercial loans to blacks pose a greater risk of default or black residential neighborhoods are more likely to decline. But this can hardly be the end of the story. What about the possibility that race conveys this information only because agents expect it to, and then act in ways that lead to the confirmation of their expectations? What if blacks have trouble getting further extensions of credit in the face of a crisis, and so default more often? Or what if nonblack residents panic at the arrival of blacks, selling their homes too quickly and below the market value to lower-income buyers, thereby promoting neighborhood decline?

If under such circumstances observers attribute racially disparate behaviors to inherent limitations of the stereotyped group—thinking, say, that blacks do not repay their loans or take care of their property because they are just less responsible people on average—these agents might well be mistaken. Yet, given that their surmise about blacks is supported by hard evidence, they might well persist in the error. Now, notice one thing: This mistake would be of great *political* moment. For attributing an endogenous difference (a difference produced within a system of interactions) to an exogenous cause (a cause located outside that system) leaves one less interested in working for systemic reform. *This* is the effect I am after with the models to be elaborated below, and this is why I am willing to employ an apparently loaded phrase like "biased social cognition": *It is a politically consequential cognitive distortion to ascribe the disadvantage to be observed among a group of people to qualities thought to be intrinsic to that group when, in fact, that disadvantage is the product of a system of social interactions.* My contention is that in American society, when the group in question is blacks, the risk of this kind of causal misattribution is especially great.

THE LOGIC OF SELF-CONFIRMING STEREOTYPES

Now, whether race is involved or not, the logic of self-confirming stereotypes as I conceive them entails three key components:

1. *rational statistical inference in the presence of limited information* (an employer, for example, wants to know how reliably and skillfully a prospective employee will work, if hired, and draws conclusions based on the data at hand—say, the employee's performance during a probationary period);

2. *feedback effects on the behavior of individuals* due to their anticipation that such inferences will be made about them (a worker, in the example, decides whether or not to acquire cer-

tain skills partly on the basis of what this worker thinks employers will conclude about him when he seeks work); and

3. *a resulting convention (economists call this an "equilibrium")* in which mutually confirming beliefs and behaviors emerge out of this interaction (the employer's surmise about his workers and the workers' decisions about skill acquisition are mutually consistent).

How can we relate this abstract way of thinking to the subject at hand? In the broadest terms, this stereotype-logic provides an analytic template to illustrate how the cognizance of race comes into existence and is reproduced through time in society. This logic, in other words, provides insight into how and why observers use *racial* categories for their classifying purposes. The point is that the inferential, self-confirming logic just outlined can easily be contingent on the *racial* characteristics of subjects, such that altogether different outcomes occur for subjects belonging to different races—that is, distinguishable by observable bodily marks. Although these race-markers may be of no intrinsic significance, they nevertheless can serve as useful indices around which human agents organize their expectations.

One way to think about race conventions, then, is to see them as the equilibria that emerge when subjects and agents in the habit of noticing certain racial markers interact with one another on matters of consequence under conditions of limited information.[8] It becomes "rational" for agents to classify a subject using functionally irrelevant (racial) markers because this allows them more accurately to assess that subject's functionally relevant but unobservable traits. Physical traits matter because observers (correctly) expect them to matter. This expectation induces agents to interact with subjects in a manner that depends on race, thereby creating different incentives for subjects in racially distinct population subgroups. Responding to these incentives, subjects adapt according to how they expect to be perceived, which is to say, they adapt differently depending on their race. In the equilibrium, this race-varying behavior by subjects is consistent (on the average) with observing agents' initial beliefs, confirming the agents' supposition that a subject's race would be informative. Race conventions emerge as by-products of the happenstance of observable morphological variability in human populations. Put differently, race matters "in the equilibrium" (as we economists would say) as a result of the inexorable logic of self-confirming feedback loops.

At this (admittedly high) level of generality, a "race" could be constructed around any cluster of inheritable physical markers shared by a largely endogamous human subpopulation that are easy for observers accurately to assess and that can be misrepresented only with difficulty. Observers, doing the best they can under trying circumstances, end up partitioning the field of human subjects in such a way that a person's hard-to-observe but functionally relevant (say, economic) traits can be effectively estimated by conditioning on that person's evidently informative though functionally irrelevant (racial) traits.

This, then, is my "model" of self-confirming racial stereotypes.

SOME ILLUSTRATIONS

We are clearly in need of examples at this point. A few thought experiments will illustrate the logic just outlined.

Imagine a group of employers who harbor the a priori belief that blacks are more likely than others to be low-effort trainees. Suppose they observe the number of mistakes any employee makes on the job, but not the effort exerted by that employee during the training period. Let employers have the option of terminating a worker during the training period, and suppose they find it much more difficult to do so later on. Then employers will set a lower threshold for blacks than for other employees on the number of mistakes needed to trigger dismissal, since, given their prior beliefs, they will be quicker to infer that a black worker has not put in enough effort to learn the job. Mistakes by black workers early in their tenure will provide evidence of the employers' worst fears, more so than an equal number of mistakes by other workers. Employers will, therefore, be less willing to extend the benefit of the doubt to blacks during the training period.

But how will black workers respond to such behavior by employers? It is costly to exert effort during the training period, and the reward for doing so can only be realized if an employee escapes termination. Knowing they are more likely to be fired if they make a few mistakes, an outcome over which they cannot exert full control, more black than other workers may find that exerting high effort during the training period is, on net, a losing proposition for them.[9] If so, fewer of them will elect to exert themselves. But this will only confirm the employers' initial beliefs, thereby bringing about a convention in which the employers' racial stereotype—"blacks tend to be low-effort trainees"—will (seem to) be entirely reasonable.

Alternatively, suppose most taxi drivers refuse to stop for young black men after a certain hour because they fear being robbed, though a few drivers will stop for anyone. Let there be two types of young men—those merely trying to get home late at night and those intent on robbery—and let us suppose that the relative number of the two types does not depend on race.[10] Now, for most young men, anticipating a long wait will discourage dependence on taxi transportation. They may arrange to ride with friends, take public transport, or bring a car, and this is especially so if a young man is simply trying to get home. But a person bent on robbery will not be so easily deterred. Even though he knows most cabs are unlikely to stop, he only needs one to do so to get in his night's work.[11] Given that taxi drivers treat blacks differently, stopping less frequently for them, and that robbers are less easily deterred than are the law abiding, the drivers' reluctance to stop will discourage relatively more of the law abiding than of the robbers among blacks from relying on taxi transportation. This effect will not be present for nonblacks, since drivers are quite willing to stop for them. Hence, through a process that economists call "adverse selection," the set of young black men actually seen to be hailing taxis after dark may well come to contain a noticeably larger than average fraction of robbers, precisely the circumstance presumed by the drivers in the first place.

Notice what is happening here: The drivers' own behaviors have created the facts on which their pessimistic expectations are grounded. Indeed, in the context of this thought experiment, were most drivers as willing to stop for young black men as for others, the set of blacks hailing cabs would be no more threatening than the overall population average. But then it would be reasonable for drivers to pay no heed to race when deciding whether or not to stop! So is it "rational," or not, for drivers to use race as a signifier of danger? Clearly, once a convention employing the self-confirming stereotype has been established, the drivers' beliefs and actions are defensible on the basis of reason. And yet the deeper conclusion—that there is an intrinsic connection between race and crime—is altogether unjustified. I think it is safe to assume that this subtle distinction will elude most cab drivers, politicians, Op-Ed writers, and not a few social scientists!

Consider another example. Suppose automobile dealers think black buyers have higher reservation prices than whites—prices above which they will simply walk away rather than haggle further. On this belief, dealers will be tougher when bargaining with blacks, more reluctant to offer low prices, more eager to foist on them expensive accessories, and so on. Now, given that such race-based behavior by dealers is common, blacks will come to expect tough dealer bargaining as the norm when they shop for cars. As such, a black buyer who contemplates walking away will have to anticipate less favorable alternative opportunities and higher search costs than will a white buyer who entertains that option. And so the typical black buyer may find it rational to accept a price rather than continue searching elsewhere, even though the typical white may reject that same price.[12] Yet this racial difference in typical behavior by buyers is precisely what justified the view among dealers that a customer's race would predict bargaining behavior. Thus, even if there are no intrinsic differences in bargaining ability between the two populations, a convention can emerge in which the dealers' rule of thumb, "be tougher with blacks," is all too clearly justified by the facts.

Here is a final example. Suppose black and white students apply for admission to a group of professional schools, and that the schools are keen to admit what they think of as an adequate number of blacks. Suppose further that, in the experience of the admissions officers at these schools, there is a substantial disparity in the academic merit of black and white applicants, on the average, and that the use of a uniform standard for the two racial groups would not yield an adequate number of black admissions. Accordingly, in order to meet their racial diversity goals, these admissions officers are convinced that they must accept some blacks with test scores and/or grades that would lead to rejection if submitted by a white applicant. Let most schools follow this policy, and consider the incentives for achievement that will have been created in the racially distinct student populations. Blacks will (correctly) anticipate that the level of performance sufficient for them to gain admission is lower than the level (correctly) presumed necessary by whites. If students are, at least to some extent, responsive to these differing incentives, then those anticipating tougher standards may (on average) exert greater effort than those anticipating more relaxed admission standards.[13] If this is so, the initial belief by admissions officers—that different standards were necessary to achieve enough diversity—may have been a self-fulfilling prophecy: There may have been no difference in the underlying tendency of the two groups of students to achieve high test scores and grades. Using race-dependent admissions standards may have set in motion a sequence of events that, in the end, confirmed in the officers' minds that their preferential handling of black applicants was required. Had the officers steadfastly stuck to racially uniform standards, they might thereby have created a factual circumstance in which their diversity goals could be met without any use of race in the admissions process.[14]

SOME GOOD QUESTIONS

At this point, a reader may be asking some questions, such as:

1. If the racial markers are truly arbitrary, then why are the blacks so often on the short end of this process? (I will call this Good Question #1.)

2. If the association between payoff-irrelevant markers and payoff-relevant traits is not intrinsic, but is engendered by the nature of agent-subject interaction, then shouldn't somebody learn what is going on and intervene to short-circuit the feedback loop producing this inequality? (Good Question #2.)

3. If knowing about unobserved traits is really so important, why don't observing agents invest in identifying other, nonracial, markers that may be equally or more informative but less racially invidious? (Good Question #3.)

4. Doesn't this kind of classificatory behavior, however reasonable or even necessary in certain circumstances, have very different effects on people who may share the same physical markers but are otherwise quite dissimilar? (Good Question #4.)

These questions go to the heart of the matter, and dealing with them leads naturally into a discussion of racial stigma. Before going further, however, I wish to make two observations.

First, I want to declare that I do not see the feedback mechanism just illustrated as the be-all and end-all of race-based behavior in society. As will become evident, I believe people attend to racial markers because they convey *social meanings,* and not just *social information.* Still, I think that to study conventional stereotyping is an empirically relevant and analytically useful exercise. It yields insight into how racially disparate outcomes can be understood without recourse to essentialist assumptions of innate racial difference. It shows how acquired differences in capabilities between members of different racial groups—due for instance to unequal access to resources critical for human development—can be magnified into even larger differences in social outcomes. It clarifies why "The data bear me out when I say 'those people' are really less productive" is no good answer to the complaint that widely disparate group outcomes should be a cause of concern for anyone interested in social justice. This way of thinking at least hints at how great the cost may be—for members of a racially marked group, to be sure, but for the entire society as well—when widely held negative stereotypes about a visibly distinct subset of the population are allowed to persist indefinitely. And it shows why broad-based, system-wide interventions may be the only way to break into the causal chain that perpetuates racial inequality over time.

Second, I want to discourage any rush to moral judgment about the behavior of observing agents (the employers, cab drivers, automobile dealers, or admissions officers) in the examples just offered. As I see it, we are dealing with deep-seated cognitive behavior here. There is no getting around classification—it is the way of the world. People will classify when the stakes are high enough. Thus, our imaginary taxi driver stands to gain $10 from a law-abiding fare but to lose, say, $10,000 on average if he stops for a robber (allowing for possible loss of life or limb). With those stakes, even if the probability of robbery is on the order of one chance in a thousand, a small difference in the behavior of racial groups may shift a driver's cost-benefit calculus from a "stop" to a "do not stop" decision. With the stakes so high, with information so limited, and given that a real correlation between "race" and "chance of robbery" is there to be observed, why should we condemn this taxi driver?

However, consider a traffic cop sitting in a $50,000 cruiser, who has received $100,000 worth of training, is backed by a big bureaucracy, and has a computer at his fingertips that allows him, by simply reading a license plate, to instantly generate reams of information. This is an observer with no excuse for allowing his behavior to be driven by racial generalizations. So my purpose here is to *analyze,* not *moralize.* I am arguing neither "for" nor "against" stereotypes. I seek merely to grasp their consequences; to fathom how racial stereotyping creates the facts that are its own justification; to understand how reasonable people, who base their surmises on hard evidence, can nonetheless hold the pernicious idea that blacks are different from others in some deeper (than race) way that accounts for their lowly status. The social production of such outcomes must first be understood. Only then, it seems to me, will it be possible to engage in effective social criticism.

But what about those good questions? I will address them in turn.

The self-confirming feedback process just illustrated treated each instance in isolation from the others, made no mention of history, and ignored factors like *prejudice* and *misinformation*—indeed, willful misinformation. Nor did it allow for any interaction between, on the one hand, reasonable information-based distinctions and, on the other hand, maltreatment of persons due to old-fashioned, unreasoning racial antipathy. And crucially, it did not ask whether persons subject to marker-based discrimination would have their ideas about their own worth or that of others with the same markers affected in any way. It is clear that, in the case of African Americans, all of these are counterfactual omissions. Taking such factors into account would, I submit, go some way toward answering Good Question #1.

Now, consider Good Question #2, which might be expanded as follows: Why don't people learn about the self-confirming feedback mechanism and intervene so as to break the production of racial stereotypes, or disrupt their reproduction through time? Why doesn't somebody do something about the entrenchment and reification of this way of thinking? If race-based classification is a human product—a social construction—then shouldn't humans be able to control it? This question goes to the core of my concerns in this book, so I will take it up at some length.

LEARNING ABOUT FEEDBACK EFFECTS

To aid in this reflection, consider the key distinction between "competitive" and "monopolistic" observing situations. A competitive situation is one in which there are a large number of observing agents, each encountering subjects from an even larger, common population, each taking actions in relation to these subjects but knowing that, owing to their relatively insignificant size, no action they can take will affect the population's characteristics. A monopolistic situation is one in which a single observing agent (or a quite small number) acts on a population of subjects. Examples of competitive observing situations include the taxi drivers encountering prospective fares and deciding whether or not to stop on the basis of their estimates of the likelihood of being robbed, and the low-wage labor market of a big city where many small employers hire from a common labor pool and use "race" as an indicator of likely worker reliability. Examples of monopolistic observing situations include a police department setting policy about how its officers should conduct traffic surveillance, the labor market in a small city where one or a few big employers dominate the hiring, and a huge bureaucracy like the military that deals with millions of people on a national scale.

Now, a monopolistic observer might upon reflection become aware of how his behavior (the use of racial markers to formulate race-dependent estimates of subjects' hard-to-observe traits) produces feedback effects in the distinct populations in a way that ends up confirming his initial beliefs. That is, a monopolistic observer might try to take into account the incentive effects sketched earlier so as to improve the equity and the efficiency of the subject-observer interactions. But this would not be possible for a competitive observer. Even if a small employer or a taxi driver learned or was told about such feedback effects, there would be nothing to be done because, in a competitive situation, an individual's action has so little impact on the overall observing environment. So Good Question #2 is most relevant in monopolistic observing situations.

This terminology—referring to "monopolistic" and "competitive" observing situations—is borrowed from economics in analogy with the distinction between sellers who do and those who do not have the power to set market prices. The analogy can be taken one step further: Even when sellers lack market power they can still act in concert, with the aid of government regulations, to set and enforce a minimum price. Likewise, in my model, even though competitive agents cannot influence the observing environment on their own, their collective action via government remains a possibility. So Good Question #2 may still be relevant in competitive observing situations, once allowance is made for the possibility of a coordinated response implemented through public policy. In any event, the question is certainly relevant in monopolistic observing situations, and these are numerous enough. So why, we must ask, do those observers who have "the power to create facts" not learn and intervene?

To venture an answer, and to hint further at the role of racial stigma in my overall argument, suppose this observer can credit two qualitative causal accounts of what produces his data. The first is the story just told, in which "race" predicts behavior only because, thinking it will do so, the observer uses the race-marker to discriminate, thereby inducing a statistical association between functionally irrelevant though easily observable marker and functionally relevant but unobservable trait. The second account posits that the marker itself is intrinsically relevant in some way. That is, the second account credits to some extent the view (racial essentialism) that I explicitly rejected in Axiom 2. Now, if a monopolistic observer believes mainly the first account, he will see the racially disparate outcome as being anomalous or surprising. He may therefore find it to be *in his own self-interest* to experiment, so as to learn about the structure that is generating his observations. He may be led in this way to reduce his reliance on the racial marker and, in so doing, to unmake the factual circumstance that initially justified its use.

However, if this monopolistic observer credits mainly the second, essentialist account, he will not see much of a benefit to be garnered from experimentation.[15] (We need not assume that the observer wholly believes one story or the other; he may think either possible. My argument works so long as the essentialist account is given sufficient weight.)

In this case, the observer's experience does more than simply confirm his beliefs; it comports with his inchoate sense of the natural order of things. "Those people just don't make good workers," he will conclude, and he will continue to view them with the skepticism that, on the unsurprising (and uninspiring) evidence at hand, they seem so richly to deserve, looking down on their feeble and ineffective strivings, to borrow a phrase from W. E. B. Du Bois, with "amused contempt and pity."

Now, a rationalistic account could be developed in which an agent experiments even though with current beliefs this seems unlikely to pay, because the agent thinks those beliefs may be wrong and realizes that experimentation may uncover the error. This, for instance, is one way that scientific communities function so as to advance the frontiers of knowledge. However, as Thomas Kuhn observed long ago, experimentation of this kind generally requires an observer to encounter events that are anomalous, challenging previously taken-for-granted understandings (Kuhn 1962). And whereas the incentives facing scientific investigators are structured precisely so as to encourage this "anomaly hunting," it is something of an understatement to observe that the incentives facing those who employ low-skilled workers or who run police departments are not so structured.

The key point here, and the answer I have for Good Question #2, is this: Learning to discard an erroneous or incomplete causal explanation in matters of race is generally not a straightforward undertaking. If, on Kuhn's account, highly disciplined scientific communities have trouble abandoning an outmoded paradigm, we may be sure that less formal social aggregates will as well. Revision of beliefs may well be a cognitive activity, but that cognition is always rooted in a social context and influenced by the taken-for-granted suppositions that agents hold.[16] As a result, if a racial disparity does not strike a powerful observer as being disturbing, anomalous, contrary to his unexamined and perhaps not even consciously espoused presumptions about the nature of his social world, then he may make no special effort to uncover a deeper (than race) cause of the disparity. Certainly, the possibility that his own behavior has helped to engender the problem will be unlikely to occur to him. However reasonable (that is, nonarbitrary, grounded in evidence) his beliefs may be, the process through which he arrives at and holds on to those beliefs need not, and generally will not, be "rational" at all.

Indeed, in the academic field of decision theory the study of how rational agents learn is an underdeveloped area of research. Moreover, a powerful critique has been made of the notion that rational choice theory can, even in principle, give a foundational account of learning. The sociologist Barry Barnes eloquently makes this case, and, since it bears importantly on my own argument here, I quote Barnes at length:

> In order to act as ER (economically rational) individuals we have to be knowledgeable. But knowledge . . . cannot be taken as given . . . Much of it has to be learned. The

problem then arises of how far learning is rational action. It arises in the most acute form in the case of the new member, just arrived in the world with very little cognitive baggage at all, about to acquire language, knowledge and culture ab initio . . . Consider an ER baby, lying in its cot facing its new world of threat and opportunity. Will it consult its preference schedule and reflect: "Well what should I do now? A restful nap perhaps, or a spot of healthy foot-kicking for muscle development. Or perhaps a cry for mother, to do a bit of language-learning. Hang on a minute! How can I be thinking this when I haven't any language yet to . . .?" New members . . . cannot be rational in quite the way that existing members perhaps are, because rationality requires mastery of a repertoire of symbols and reference to a body of knowledge, neither of which new members possess. The activities of new members, therefore, and in particular their learning activities, pose a special challenge to an individualist social theory with which they are prima facie incompatible . . . Evidently acts of learning, classification and inference . . . raise pervasive problems for individualism . . . It would seem that individuals must act in a certain sense arbitrarily if they are to act at all; what is routinely identified as rational action begins to look as if it is conventional action. (Barnes 1995, 34–36)

RACE AND SOCIAL COGNITION

Barry Barnes makes a good point that applies far beyond the confines of a nursery or a playpen: We cannot hope to explain all of human behavior with a cost-benefit calculus.

Specifically, when we ask how people acquire the mechanisms of symbolic expression peculiar to the communities in which they are embedded, we must consider the meaning of their relations with others. Plausibly, much social learning will come about as a by-product of social activity undertaken for its own sake: One wants to get along in the world, in this community, with other people. So one undertakes to see the world as others do—not because the benefit of doing so outweighs the cost, but because that is the way of being in the world with these people. This kind of thinking suggests that it is futile to look for "rationality" at the foundation of all social action.

But although Barnes's critique is powerful, we need not adopt so comprehensive a view to appreciate a key point. We can stick with a more or less rational account of learning, and simply observe that people have to take a "cognitive leap of faith" with respect to how they specify the environment in which their learning is to take place. That choice of specification, plausibly, cannot be a fully rational act. Intuitively, the cognition underlying it is more a "pattern recognition" than a "deductive" type of cognition. It is as if the agent is thinking: "This fits. This feels about right. I think this framing of the problem is more or less accurate. Now, having so framed, I will go on to make a deductive calculation about whether this or that alternative hypothesis, seen from within my adopted frame of reference, makes sense."

I admit that this is far from a rigorous social-psychological argument. I am aware that, by advancing it, I step rather far out on the proverbial limb. But as the force of Good Question #2 makes clear, some speculation of this sort is warranted, given the stakes. For if agents do not learn about mechanisms within their control that reproduce racial inequality through time, the results may be tragic. Consider the possibility that learning about the ultimate (not proximate) causes of a group disparity fails to occur for one division of the population (black/white) because, when told that the blacks are lagging, people's sense is: "They are about where we expected them to be." But learning does take place for a different division of the population (male/female) because, upon hearing that the girls are lagging, people instinctively harbor the thought: "Something must be dreadfully wrong."

This is no simple accusation of "racism." Nor am I charging the American people with caring more about gender inequality than about racial inequality—though it may be that they do so. Rather, I am making what I take to be a pertinent observation about the cognitive-adaptive possibilities implicit in various social situations, in which observers try to discern how the facts on which they base their decisions have been generated.

Specifically, I want to distinguish two cognitive acts required to process social information—*specification* and *inference.* An observer first adopts a *specification,* within the framework of which an *inference* is subsequently drawn. Specification refers to the *qualitative* framework guiding an agent's data processing. Inference refers to the *quantitative* calculation of parameters from available data. The language is borrowed from statistics but is intended to apply to the cognitive assessments of ordinary persons, not statisticians.

Now, I assert that the mental processes underlying these cognitive acts are fundamentally different, and that while inference may be well conceived as a fully rational enterprise, specification is best thought of as an intuitive, instinctual, pattern-recognition type of activity. The cognition underlying the self-confirming feedback loops that lead to racial stereotypes, as illustrated in the foregoing thought experiments, is an instance of *inference.* But the questioning of long-held beliefs, and the willingness to experiment for the sake of learning though this might seem not to pay—these are instances of *specification.* We should expect nonrational factors—in particular, the taken-for-granted meanings that may be unreflectively associated with certain racial markers—to exert a significant influence on the latter type of cognitive behavior.

Here, then, is my final answer to Good Question #2: "Race" may be a human product, but, because it is a social convention that emerges out of the complex interactions of myriad, autonomous decision-makers, it is not readily subjected to human agency. Between us reflective agents and our social artifacts stand mechanisms of social intercourse that are anything but transparent. Because we filter social experience through racial categories, and given the ancillary meanings with which those categories are freighted, we can be led to interpret our data in such a way that the arbitrariness of the race convention remains hidden from our view, leaving us "cognitive prisoners" inside a symbolic world of our own unwitting construction.

BECOMING "STREETWISE"

I conclude this chapter by considering Good Questions #3 and #4. Why don't observers look for nonracial markers to solve their inference problems? And what ensues when people who happen to share some markers are, willy-nilly, grouped into a single racial category, and yet those so grouped are objectively very different persons? Obviously, these two questions are closely related: The more heterogeneous is a racial group, the greater is the gain to an observer from using nonracial markers.

But we have already discussed this problem; looking for nonracial markers is merely another way of experimenting with one's specification of the process generating one's data. It is, in the colloquialism made famous by the University of Pennsylvania sociologist Elijah Anderson, a way of being "streetwise" (Anderson 1990). I will employ Anderson's framework to make a final point about racial stereotypes.

Adapting the theory first elaborated by Erving Goffman (1959), Anderson uses the streets of the racially mixed West Philadelphia neighborhoods near the campus of the University of Pennsylvania as a laboratory. He studies the problem of "decoding" which all social actors must solve when meeting others in public. One cannot be entirely certain of the character or intent of "the other"; it is necessary to process such information as may be gleaned from an examination of the external self-presentation of those being encountered. The context of the meeting—time of day, physical setting, whether the individual is alone or in a group, and so on—will affect how these external clues are read. As an encounter unfolds, communication between the parties, ranging from a meeting of eyes (or the avoidance of same) to an exchange of greetings, permits further inferences to be drawn. Race—an easily and instantly ascertainable characteristic—may, as I have suggested, be expected to play a large role in this game of inference. Social class—as conveyed by dress, manner, occupation, and speech—may also be quite important. (In fact, as Anderson's account makes clear, these two indicia of social identity interact in subtle and complex ways.) An individual's experience of the social environment is strongly influenced by how he and those he encounters in public negotiate such meetings.

Anderson describes in elegant detail the rules of public etiquette, norms of mutual expectation, conventions of deference, methods of self-protection, strategies of turf-claiming, signals of intention, deciphering of cues, mistakes, biases, bluffs, threats, and self-fulfilling prophecies that are implicit in the interactions he observes. His ethnography is a wonderful illustration (indeed, a *vindication*) of the theoretical approach I am promoting in this book. He identifies social roles, public routines, and behavioral devices common to the encounters he chronicles. And he suggests compelling explanations for many puzzling features of life on the streets of the communities he has studied.

Anderson's core concept in this work is the notion of becoming "streetwise," meaning adept at subtly decoding the markers presented to one in the streets. At the crudest level, a resident uses race, or possibly race combined with class, as a key indicator of danger (or of opportunity, depending on what the observer is on the lookout for). But on Anderson's account streetwise persons advance beyond this crude level, becoming shrewder at navigating the streets, thereby enabling themselves to sustain deeper and more meaningful relationships across the racial divide. An observer becomes streetwise by experimenting with nonracial markers, or perhaps more accurately, by supplementing racial markers with a wide array of nonracial ones that refine the discriminatory practice and permit more nuance in the treatment of those bearing a negative racial marker. Thus the white lady who runs into her apartment as soon as she sees a black kid approaching from across the street, clutching her bag close, looking furtively over her shoulder, is not "streetwise." She hasn't bothered to take any note of the signs: Is the kid carrying a book under his arm? How is he dressed? What are his gait and demeanor? She hasn't learned about other, nonracial information that might be powerfully informative in that particular situation. "Street wisdom" is just a generalization of that remark.

This behavior—acquiring street wisdom—is surely commendable, one would think. We might all hope (and pray?) that those authorized to use deadly force on America's city streets will soon acquire greater wisdom in this regard. But notice one thing. By eschewing stereotype-driven behavior and using a more refined set of indices to guide their discrimination, observers encourage the production of those very indices of differentiation by better-off members of the negatively stereotyped group, because they are the ones who gain most by separating themselves from the masses.[17] I do not say here that this is necessarily a bad thing, though I can easily imagine circumstances in which it would be.

The strategies of social identity manipulation used by racially marked people to inhibit being stereotyped—their methods of "partial passing"—are endless: affectations of speech; dressing up to shop at a downtown store; writing more equations on the blackboard than needed, to show a skeptical audience that one does indeed have complete command of the discipline's technical apparatus; "whistling Vivaldi" while walking along a city's mean streets so as not to be mistaken for a thug[18]—most generally, adopting styles of self-presentation that aim to communicate "I'm not one of THEM; I'm one of YOU!" Such differentiating behavior can undermine a pernicious equilibrium in which the use of an intrinsically irrelevant racial trait has become institutionalized as a social convention.

But such strategies can also be a way to undermine solidarity in the race-marked population, and to encourage the selective out-migration (through subtle forms of "partial passing") of the most talented. And they can promote a fractured ego, an insider's own-group antipathy—"if only THEY would get their acts together, then people like ME wouldn't have such a problem"—which is anything but pretty. When this process results in the pursuit of social mobility in a racially marked group by means of directed marriage patterns intended to preserve lightened skin tones over the generations (a commonplace of African-American society in years gone by which has yet to fully dissipate, and which can be found in Brazilian society even today); or when the better-off classes of the racially marked indulge themselves by preening obsessively over minute symbols of their relatively superior status (as the sociologist E. Franklin Frazier described nearly a half-century ago; Frazier 1957), the nature of the problem becomes apparent.

I wish to avoid misunderstanding. I do not intend these remarks to be an attack on the act of "partial passing" as such. Nor do I see that act as some kind of immoral betrayal. But neither can I celebrate it blithely as a glorious exercise in individual liberty, or as a god-sent mechanism for subverting an otherwise oppressive racial order. To the contrary, the tragedy of the selective out-migration of a relative few from the marked population through partial passing is that it places the burden of reforming a racially stereotypic order on those with little leverage to alter underlying social structures (letting our monopolistic observers off the hook). And, perhaps more importantly though certainly more speculatively, it promotes a liberal individualist ideology of personal achievement that reinforces, rather than challenges, an order in which the scourge of racial stigma can flourish.

So I hold there to be nothing wrong with individuals doing their best under trying circumstances by "passing" out of their stigmatized racial group through artful acts of selective self-presentation. Those doing so are not rightly indicted as reactionaries. But by the same token their behavior is unlikely to provide much political inspiration.

LOOKING AHEAD

With these speculations in view, the key role that racial stigma plays in my argument should now be easier to see. In the next chapter I propose that durable racial inequality be understood as the outgrowth of a series of "vicious circles of cumulative causation." The story goes something like this: The "social meaning of race"—that is, the tacit understandings associated with "blackness" in the public's imagination, especially the negative connotations—biases the social cognitions and distorts the specifications of observing agents, inducing them to make causal misattributions detrimental to blacks. Observers have difficulty identifying with the plight of a people whom they mistakenly assume simply to be "reaping what they have sown." This lack of empathy undermines public enthusiasm for egalitarian racial reform, thus encouraging the reproduction through time of racial inequality. Yet, absent such reforms, the low social conditions of (some) blacks persist, the negative social meanings ascribed to blackness are thereby reinforced, and so the racially biased social-cognitive processes are reproduced, completing the circle. As they navigate through the epistemological fog, observing agents find their cognitive sensibilities being influenced by history and culture, by social conditions, and by the continuing construction and transmission of civic narrative. Groping along, these observers—acting in varied roles, from that of economic agent to that of public citizen—"create facts" about race, even as they remain blind to their ability to unmake those facts and oblivious to the moral implications of their handiwork.

Calling this behavior racism, while doing little violence to the language, also fails to produce much insight. How, we should ask, will this self-reinforcing process be contested? Epithets are unlikely to be of much help. Subtle dynamics underlie racially biased social cognition—dynamics that are not much illuminated when conceived as some form of anti-black enmity. Note, for instance, that the argument to this point has made no reference to the race of the observer. Whereas a theory grounded in racial enmity would have trouble explaining anti-black sentiments held by other blacks, nothing in my theory prevents a black from succumbing to the same cognitive biases as anyone else, when drawing inferences about the underlying causes of racial inequality. Nor would I dismiss the possibility that perceptions by blacks of the larger society—of the opportunities available to them for upward mobility, for instance—might be distorted by racially conditioned causal misattributions on their part.

Here is yet another reason to resist the temptation to moralize when discussing these issues. *I hold that it is more fruitful to focus on the cognitive rather than the normative aspects of this problem, attending to how people—often unreflectively—think about social information.* So, anyway, I hope to persuade the reader with the argument to follow.

3

RACIAL STIGMA

I HAVE JUST argued that human beings are hungry for information, that we partially sate this hunger by attending to the bodily markings of those whom we encounter in society, and that this nearly universal practice—the forming of generalizations based on superficial physical traits by decision-making agents with the power to create facts—can have politically profound and morally disturbing consequences. But that is only part of the story. We humans are also hungry for meanings. As the sociologist Pierre Bourdieu has cleverly observed, "the experience of meaning is part and parcel of the total meaning of experience" (Bourdieu and Wacquant 1992, p. 9). If navigating our way through the social fog is a problem, that is only because we have goals, purposes, ultimate ends. We strive to "transcend the world of existences," in Vaclav Havel's lovely phrase—to impute an ineffable significance to the artifacts that furnish our lives. In what follows I hope to show that considering the experience of *racial* meaning is necessary if we are to grasp fully the meaning of racial inequality as it is now experienced in American society.

Because human beings look for and derive meaning from the material substratum in which we are embedded, human behavior is determined not only by material and institutional structures but also by what those structures are understood to signify. The arbitrary bodily marks associated with racial distinction are among the structures in our social environment to which meanings about the identity, capability, and worthiness of their bearers have been imputed. I repeat: "Race" is all about embodied social signification. In this sense, it is a *social truth* that race is quite real, despite what may be the *biologic-taxonomic truth* of the claim that there are no races. Recognizing this social truth is critical to the project at hand. For the social meanings imputed to race-symbols have had profound, enduring, and all-too-real consequences—consequences due not to any race-dependent biological processes but rather to a system of race-dependent meanings, habitual social significations, that can be more difficult to "move" than that proverbial, all-too-material mountain.

So, having made the economist's case about information, incentives, and racial reputations, I now look at racial stigma in order to expand horizons. These morphological features—associated in a society at an historical moment with what are taken to be the races—are more than mere forecasting tools. Nor are they simply ciphers facilitating a more or less accurate reading of a person's unseen traits. They are also signs from which cues of identity are drawn, and upon which indices of belongingness are inscribed. As we encounter one another in social space, we perceive the physical markings on one another's bodies and go on to play our respective parts, enacting scripts written long before we were born. It is hard not to notice these racial signs, difficult not to be moved in any way by them. We are confused or discomforted when confronted by someone who does not fit our categories. We search for an inoffensive way to resolve the ambiguity—to discover whether she thinks of herself as being black or white, Asian or Hispanic. This ought not to matter, we tell ourselves, for how we approach her, for where we see her fitting into our lives—and yet, all too often, the potential for sociability is circumscribed by instantaneous, visceral reactions to the race-markers of the other. Here, I maintain, is a key feature of our problem. For when that "other" being encountered in American society is black, and when there is a question of her fitness for intimacy, taboos and suspicions—long in the making, and difficult to acknowledge or confront—come quickly to the fore. This is no longer the taxi driver's problem—the evidently justified fear of harassment or worse. Here we enter the territory of *racial stigma,* of dishonorable meanings socially inscribed on arbitrary bodily marks, of "spoiled collective identities."

GOFFMAN'S "STIGMA" AND MINE

As mentioned, I approach "racial stigma" via the work of Erving Goffman (1963). In his book *Stigma: Notes on the Management of Spoiled Identity,* Goffman studies the problems faced by people with virtual social identities that are disreputable or "spoiled"—people carrying bodily marks (stigmata) that incline others to judge them negatively, but also people with less visible markings who live at constant risk of being "exposed." So Goffman's stigmatized were the blind, the deaf, the "cripple," the drunk, the ex–mental patient, the homosexual.

Taking his analysis as a point of departure, I wish to emphasize one of Goffman's central distinctions: between an identity constructed "from the outside," via social imputations based on a person's physical presentation, and an identity constructed "from the inside," via the accumulation of facts specific to a person's biography. The former is virtual, a social artifact, a construction that reflects whatever social meanings may be ascribed to the visible marks. The latter is actual, a life history, something relatively objective, more or less independent of conventional ascriptions. These two identities—the virtual and the actual ones—can diverge systematically in the social experience of a given individual. And when this happens, an interesting drama unfolds for both subject and observer. This is Erving Goffman's key insight, which I borrow to enrich this reflection on racial inequality.

Let the virtual social identity imputed to a subject be negative, because observers tend to associate the visible indicators at hand with some dishonorable conception of the subject. Then, following Goffman, this person's social identity is "spoiled" in an essential way, and it can rightly be said that the person is "stigmatized." Moreover, and crucially, this stigmatization is not merely the drawing of a negative surmise about someone's productive attributes. It entails doubting the person's worthiness and consigning him or her to a social netherworld. Indeed, although the language is somewhat hyperbolic, it means being skeptical about whether the person can be assumed to share a common humanity with the observer. Drawing on this observation, and calling to mind the legacy of racial dishonor engendered by the history of chattel slavery in the United States, I want to suggest that the idea of "racial stigma" can be used to gain insight into problems of perception, representation, and standing in contemporary American public life that adversely affect (some) blacks.

To make this point with greater precision, let us consider another thought experiment—called to mind by the problem of racial profiling. Imagine that there are two alternative possible states of affairs: In Situation 1 a race-marked subgroup is homogeneous; each member engages in a criminal activity on any occasion with a probability of, say, one in ten. In Situation 2 the group is heterogeneous; 90 percent are "good guys" who never engage in any criminal activity, and 10 percent are "bad guys" who always do. The two situations are extreme, bracketing assumptions about the degree of homogeneity characteristic of a racially identifiable subgroup of the population that, in the aggregate and on every occasion, offends against some criminal stricture at a 10 percent rate.

Distinguishing between these situations is important. Situation 1 may afford some justification for the practice of racial profiling; but that practice is harder to justify in Situation 2. This is because profiling entails two kinds of error: false positives (stopping the innocent) and false negatives (not stopping the guilty). The relative cost of making these two types of error varies with the situation. Thus, in Situation 1, members of the target group are all equally guilty—each, though possibly innocent on a given occasion, breaks the law 10 percent of the time. Detaining habitual offenders who happen not to have offended this time (let's call this "rounding up the usual suspects") well may be seen as a price worth paying to ensure that the real violator does not get away. In Situation 2, on the other hand, 90 percent of the target group never offends. In this case, a prudent decision-maker well might think that allowing the perpetually offending minority within the group to pass unmolested is a price worth paying to avoid harassing the perpetually innocent majority. So it is not implausible to hold that profiling is only justified when the police are convinced that the true state of affairs approximates Situation 1.

Now, let us suppose that in actual fact Situation 2 obtains, but that a law enforcement agent erroneously believes Situation 1 to be the correct specification. The agent thinks, "If they look alike they act alike," when nothing could be further from the truth. Let this agent on each occasion observe the behavior of a randomly chosen subject from the population, and let him be informed about the aggregate rate of criminal offending. Notice that, no matter what this agent observes for any single individual with whom he has contact, he never changes his beliefs, either about the aggregate offending rate for the group or about the extent to which the offending behavior is generalized within the group. He will learn that his specification of the degree of homogeneity is wildly off only if he invests in tracking his experience over time with particular individuals, *identifying them in some way that is more specific than the gross racial marker,* and retaining historical evidence about the frequency distribution of offenses in the racially defined subpopulation. He must, in other words, attend to their *actual* and not only their *virtual* identities. Were he to plot the relevant histograms (number of persons in the group who, over some period of time, are observed to commit no offense, one offense, two offenses, and so on), he would see that his specification is wrong; otherwise, nothing he observes will be inconsistent with his initial presumptions. Although "usual suspects" should be defined by their criminal biographies, this agent will persist in defining them by their racial morphologies.

So uncovering specification error in this example—learning that a group's average behavior is a poor predictor of what to expect from almost everyone in the group—requires a law enforcement agent to avoid constructing his subjects' social identities "from the outside." But, and this is crucial, given his initial beliefs, he will expect it to be a waste of time and resources to retain idiosyncratic data. He perceives little gain from distinguishing individuals because he begins with the conviction that they are all alike. And yet unless he tracks individuals he cannot learn that he is dead wrong in this presumption. If he is not forced to track individuals then, short of a coincidental sequence of fortuitous encounters, he is likely to persist in his erroneous belief and act accordingly. That is, *he doesn't learn because he doesn't think learning will pay. This judgment is firmly rooted, however, in his ignorance. Unless he is willing to experiment, to test the limits of his prior generalization as a matter of principle, he will retain his false belief.*

This possibility, the reader will recall, was brought to light in the previous chapter in the discussion of our Good (old) Question #2. Will the police department experiment with its specification, or not? It depends, I am arguing here, on just what virtual social identities are imputed to the people subject to these powerful discretionary acts. My claim, to be defended at length, is that when the subjects are racially stigmatized, the prospects for such learning are sharply diminished.

Therefore, the angle of vision employed by our hypothetical police officer when he encounters race-marked citizens is of some significance. As race-markers come to be more salient and to be freighted with powerful social meanings, the odds diminish that an observer, starting with a mistaken view of a racial group, will process social information in a manner that exposes the error and leads him away from reliance on the racial trait. So we have here another vicious circle: Race becomes an important aspect of a subject's virtual social identity just when his actual identity is unknown to the observer. Yet given the convention of attending to race and the evident value of doing so, and given that the social meanings carried by the race-markers support the deleterious, homogeneous view, an observer may see no reason to track the personal life history that defines a subject's actual identity. In the event, and ironically, the subject becomes an "invisible man" precisely because of the visibility, and the social meaning, of his stigmata. It behooves us, therefore, to inquire about the source of these social meanings and their connection to the race conventions operative in American society.

RACE AND SOCIAL MEANING

How, one might ask, does a society of raced agents come over time to invest what are, after all, arbitrary physical markers—indices with no intrinsic connection to human abilities, hopes and fears, worthiness and dignity—with so much emotive power? That is, why do people cry, or die, because of meanings they associate with race-related experience? This is a deep question to which I cannot provide a comprehensive answer here. But an analogy may be helpful: What could be more arbitrary than the coordinating convention, stop on "red" and go on "green"? It would surely work just as well the other way around—stop on "green" and go on "red." The particular colors being used here can have no intrinsic significance. Still, it is not difficult to imagine that, in time, "red" might (for meaning-hungry human agents) become imbued with a sense of prohibition, and "green" with a sense of license. Once this were so, it would then be difficult to use those symbols in any other way, despite the arbitrariness of their initial designation.

So here we have a case—admittedly artificial—in which arbitrary markers nevertheless become vested with meanings that stubbornly resist change and that, when widely shared in society, place objective limits on the range of feasible social actions. But we need not look only to artificial cases. It is a commonplace of social life that accidents of time and geography—our dates or places of birth, for instance—become infused with an abiding significance, leaving us feeling connected in some way to other people with whom we may share little more than some happenstance of common origins. In analogous fashion, the symbols we call "race" have through time been infused with social meanings bearing on the identity, the status, and the humanity of those who carry them.

Once established, these meanings can come to be taken for granted, enduring unchallenged for generations. In a hierarchical society, a correspondence may develop between a person's social position and the physical marks taken in that society to signify race. Bodily signs that trigger in an observer's mind the sense that their bearer is ordained to be "a hewer of wood and drawer of water," or is a member of a "master race destined to rule the world," or is a "social pariah best avoided at all costs" illustrate the possibilities.

When the meanings connoted by race-symbols undermine an observing agent's ability to see their bearer as a person possessing a common humanity with the observer—as "someone not unlike the rest of us"—then I will say that this person is "racially stigmatized," and that the group to which he belongs suffers a "spoiled collective identity."

IN DEFENSE OF AXIOM 3

But in what sense can "blackness"—by which I mean the racial designation of African Americans—be taken to be a "spoiled collective identity"? I begin by noting that race conventions have evolved in the circumstances of time and place peculiar to a given society. This race-making was a different process on the North American continent in the seventeenth and eighteenth centuries than it was at the southern tip of the African continent in the eighteenth and nineteenth centuries, and so on. Accordingly, when considering the social meaning of race in the United States, one wants to attend to the specific historical processes that conditioned our nation's race-making. Fundamental in this regard, I assert, was the institution of chattel slavery, an institution grounded in America's primordial racial classification—the "social otherness" of blacks.

This assertion was formalized in my Axiom 3, which postulated an ingrained racial stigma adversely affecting blacks. Of the three axioms that I have offered, this one is likely to be the most controversial. Invoking the specter of slavery in a discussion of contemporary racial inequality will raise eyebrows. ("That was a long time ago," I hear the skeptics saying.) And yet, as the argument to this point makes clear, much rests on my conviction that the history of slavery in America casts a long shadow, one with contemporary relevance. So it is worthwhile to offer now some motivation for my decision to adopt Axiom 3.

In his profound treatise *Slavery and Social Death,* the historical sociologist Orlando Patterson has argued that one cannot understand slavery without grasping the importance of *honor* (Patterson 1982). Slavery, he states, is a great deal more than an institution allowing property-in-people. It is "the permanent, violent domination of natally alienated[1] and generally dishonored persons." By surveying this institution across five continents over two millennia, Patterson shows that the hierarchy of social standing—masters over slaves, reinforced by ritual and culture—is what distinguishes slavery from any other system of forced labor. This is a parasitic relationship within the social body: Masters derive honor from their virtually unlimited power over slaves, who are radically marginalized because their very social existence is wholly dependent on relations with their masters. In the

American context, obviously, the rituals and customs supporting this hierarchical order—the system of taken-for-granted meanings that made possible an adherence to high Enlightenment ideals in the midst of widespread human bondage—came to be closely intertwined in both the popular and the elite culture with ideas about race. As such, *dishonor,* shown so brilliantly by Patterson to be a general and defining feature of slavery, became, in the (American) case at hand, inseparable from the social meaning of race.

So my syllogism is this: In general, slaves are always profoundly dishonored persons. In the experience of the United States, slavery was a thoroughly racial institution. Therefore, the social meaning of race emergent in American political culture at mid-nineteenth century was closely connected with the slaves' dishonorable status. True, "that was a long time ago." And true, many Americans have great-great-grandparents who were profoundly dishonored. My point, to be illustrated momentarily, is that black Americans are exceptional in the extent to which remnants of this ignoble history are still discernible in the nation's present-day public culture.

Now if, with Patterson, we can see in American slavery not merely a legal convention but also ritual and custom defining and legitimating an order of racial hierarchy, then we should also be able to see that emancipation—the termination of the masters' legal claims—could, in itself, never be sufficient to make slaves and their progeny into full members of society. The *racial dishonor* of the former slaves and their descendants, historically engendered and culturally reinforced, would have also to be overcome. I claim that an honest assessment of current American politics—its debates about welfare, crime, schools, jobs, taxes, housing, test scores, diversity, urban policy, and much more—reveals the lingering effects of this historically engendered dishonor.

By "racial dishonor" I mean something specific: an entrenched if inchoate presumption of inferiority, of moral inadequacy, of unfitness for intimacy, of intellectual incapacity, harbored by observing agents when they regard the race-marked subjects. Axiom 3 asserts that this specter of "social otherness," of racial dishonor that emerged with slavery and that has been shaped over the post-emancipation decades by political, economic, and cultural forces specific to American society, remains yet to be fully eradicated.

So my use of the term "racial stigma" alludes to this lingering residue in post-slavery American political culture of the dishonor engendered by racial slavery. It is crucial to understand that this is not mainly an issue of the *personal attitudes* of individual Americans. To reject my argument here with the claim that "stigma cannot be so important because attitude surveys show a continued decline in expressed racism among Americans over the decades" is to thoroughly misunderstand me. I am discussing *social meanings*, not *attitudes*—specifically the meanings conveyed by race-related public actions and events. I am also invoking what might be called the "etiquette of public discourse" or, as the sociologist John David Skrentny[2] puts it, the "boundaries of legitimacy" that constrain politicians when they formulate and justify the policies they advocate. I have in mind the unexamined beliefs that influence how citizens understand and interpret the images they glean from the larger social world. I am claiming that the meaning of a policy—job preferences, say—is quite sensitive to the race of those affected: Veterans are acceptable beneficiaries but blacks violate meritocratic principles. I assert that public responses to a social malady—drug involvement, say—depend on the race of those suffering the problem: The youthful city-dwelling drug sellers elicit a punitive response, while the youthful suburban-dwelling drug buyers call forth a therapeutic one.

Nothing in these examples, I claim, turns on the racial *attitudes* of the typical American. Everything depends, I am arguing, on racially biased social cognitions that cause some situations to appear anomalous, disquieting, contrary to expectation, worthy of further investigation, inconsistent with the natural order of things—while other situations appear normal, about right, in keeping with what one might expect, consistent with the social world as we know it. These cognitive distinctions tend to be drawn to the detriment of millions of racially stigmatized citizens, I assert, because of the taint of dishonor that is part and parcel of the social meaning of race in the United States. Now, I may be right or I may be wrong about this, but no attitude survey can decide the issue.

One easily loses track of this difference between racial attitudes and racial meanings. Consider the "mere mention" experiment made famous by the Stanford political scientist Paul Sniderman and his colleagues (Sniderman and Piazza 1993). Here a group of survey researchers discover that "the mere mention" of affirmative action, in the context of soliciting from white respondents their views about racial stereotypes, makes those whites more likely to agree with negative racial generalizations like "most blacks are lazy." (In a comparison of two groups of similar whites, the ones to whom affirmative action was "merely mentioned" showed a significantly higher tendency to affirm the negative stereotypes about blacks than did those to whom affirmative action was not mentioned at all.) The researchers concluded that the respondents' expression of these anti-black sentiments had been "caused" by their dislike of affirmative action, and not the other way around. That is, whites were mainly expressing their ideological views about policy, which, upon mention of affirmative action, then spilled over to affect their views about race. The argument being developed here suggests this may be an incomplete interpretation. After all, is there any other group of beneficiaries from some controversial public policy about whom it could be true that merely mentioning the policy would trigger the affirmation of crude stereotypes in reference to the group—farmers, the elderly, the handicapped, union members, feminists, gun owners? The whites in Sniderman's experiments may, as he argues, have been driven mainly by ideology, and not by racial animus. However, it remains the case that the ideological *meanings* of a contested racial policy like affirmative action are determined within a social-cognitive matrix that is raced. A similar policy with a different set of beneficiaries might not have the same ideological resonance. More generally, if when assessing a policy observers make use of a causal specification that has been "colored" by racial stigma, then they may perceive that policy as being especially threatening to their ideological positions. With an alternative specification of the underlying social processes, that policy may not be so threatening.

RACIAL STIGMA AT WORK IN AMERICA

Obviously, slavery has not been the only historical event relevant to the making of racial stigma. Social perceptions of racial worth have also been shaped by more recent events; they have been influenced by the so-called pathological behaviors often associated with the so-called black underclass. And they have been reinforced, to be sure, by what some conservative commentators delight in referring to as "black failure."

But, while racial stigma has been encouraged in the post-slavery era by the "disreputable" behaviors observed among some blacks, it is also true that those behaviors have in some measure been influenced by racial stigma. This is the tragedy of the vicious circle. When we hear a person declare, "I disdain and avoid (some) blacks for good reasons," we do well to bear in mind that those "good reasons" emerged from a system of social interactions, a key feature of which is the tendency of a great many people to "disdain and avoid (some) blacks."

Moreover, while the stigmatized "racial other" in our midst today is unlikely to be wearing a business suit or an athlete's uniform—more probably he is wearing an inmate's jumpsuit or she an indigent, pregnant teenager's hospital gown—this observation does nothing to refute my claim that, where stigma arises, the negative social meanings associated with blackness are central to its operation. I have no need here for the exaggerated and indefensible assumption that stigma hampers social advancement for all blacks—universally and to the same degree.

Still, one ought not to presume black businessmen and athletes to be immune from the effects of racial stigma. Of course, many black athletes are revered figures in American popular culture. Their fame and marketability could easily incline one to the conclusion that no racial taint affects them. But this surmise is not warranted. Again, the distinction between racial attitudes and the social meaning of race must be borne in mind. The very same fans who idolize a black superstar—because of his athletic virtuosity and despite his race—may, upon hearing news about the criminal acts of a few well-paid miscreants, find their enthusiasm waning for the sport as a whole. The perception by nonracist fans that the sport has been "tainted" by the drug use, violence, or misogyny of a few bad actors may well reflect racial stigma, at least in part: The bad actors are mostly black and their offenses remind fans of what they most loathe and fear about "ghetto culture."

Those who run professional sports in the United States appear to be aware of this danger. Thus in August 2000 National Football League Commissioner Paul Tagliabue announced that he would levy a $250,000 fine on the Baltimore Ravens player Ray Lewis. (Lewis had acknowledged lying to police about his role in a stabbing incident that resulted in the deaths of two men, though Lewis was not the assailant.) Commissioner Tagliabue pledged to impose another $250,000 fine if Lewis were to violate the terms of his probation. In a written statement explaining his actions, Tagliabue said that he was protecting the collective reputation of all players in the league: "When an N.F.L. player engages in and admits to misconduct of the type to which Mr. Lewis has pled here, the biggest losers are thousands of other N.F.L. players, present, past and future. Such admitted misconduct clearly contributes to the negative stereotyping of N.F.L. players" (Freeman 2000, p. D8). The Commissioner's concerns would appear to be quite reasonable, and his actions can be justified under the circumstances. It is worth noting, though, in keeping with the argument of this book, that two other factors are at work here—the changing racial make-up of professional football (blacks in the last two decades have come to dominate the sport), and the fact that nearly all of the very few miscreants are (like Lewis himself) black. These factors have probably encouraged the "negative stereotyping of N.F.L. players," by associating them in fans' minds with the general taint that is racial stigma in American society.[3] I now offer some evidence of this broader problem.

Consider some basic facts about race and social intercourse in the United States. According to the 1990 Census of the Population, among married persons 25–34 years old in 1990, some 70 percent of Asian women, 39 percent of Hispanic women, but only 2 percent of black women had white Anglo husbands (Farley 1996). Talk about the threat of "black crime" and the scourge of "black illegitimacy" is a staple of call-in radio shows. Racially mixed church congregations are rare enough to make front-page news. So culturally isolated are black ghetto-dwelling teenagers that scholars find convergence in their speech patterns over great geographic distances, even as this emergent dialect grows increasingly dissimilar from the speech of poor whites living but a few miles away.[4] Childless white couples travel to Colombia and China in search of infants to adopt, while ghetto-born orphans go parentless.[5] When geographers study the spatial distribution of populations in the larger northeastern and midwestern cities, they find clusters of African Americans within a few miles of one another, in seas of despair, surrounded by the richest middle class on earth.[6]

This litany is not meant as an indictment of American society for being irredeemably racist. But it does illustrate how deeply embedded in the consciousness of this nation is the racial "otherness" of blacks. And it gives some idea of the way stigma can circumscribe opportunities for (some) blacks to develop their personal capacities, to become more integrated into society, and thus to diminish their own stigmatization.

The social isolation and negative perception of urban ghettos is a leading example of racial stigma at work in America today. These black ghetto dwellers are a people apart, ridiculed for their cultural styles, isolated socially, experiencing an internalized sense of despair, with limited access to communal networks of mutual assistance. The purported criminality, sexual profligacy, and intellectual inadequacy of these people are the frequent objects of public derision. It does not require enormous powers of perception to see how this symbolic degradation ties in with the history of race relations in the United States. The sociologist Loic Wacquant of the University of California at Berkeley has provided an apt account—based on his observations and interviews with the residents of a low-income Chicago neighborhood—of exactly what I have in mind here:

> In America, the dark ghetto stands similarly as the national symbol of urban "pathology" and its accelerating deterioration since the racial uprisings of the mid-1960s is widely regarded as incontrovertible proof of the moral dissolution, cultural depravity and behavioral deficiencies of its inhabitants . . . Today, living in the historic Black Belt of Chicago carries an automatic presumption of social unworthiness and moral inferiority which translates into an acute consciousness of the symbolic degradation associated with being confined to a loathed and despised universe. Over and beyond the scornful gaze of outsiders

> and the reality of exclusion from participation in society's regular institutions, the thoroughly depressed state of the local economy and ecology exerts a pervasive effect of demoralization upon ghetto residents . . . For the ghetto is not simply a spatial entity, or a mere aggregation of poor families stuck at the bottom of the class structure: it is a uniquely racial formation that spawns a society-wide web of material and symbolic associations between color, place and a host of negatively valued social properties. (Wacquant 1993, pp. 371–373)

The historical processes that produced these urban black ghettos graphically illustrate how racial stigma, operating over the course of the late nineteenth and early twentieth centuries, helped create the facts that are its own justification. Consider that, at the turn of the twentieth century, with millions of (black) American peasants waiting in the wings, there occurred a rapid expansion of the industrial economy in the North. Due to a complex set of social and economic relations between the peasants and southern landowners, and to the disproportionate political influence of the latter in the U.S. Congress, we ended up with peasants from Eastern and Southern Europe being drawn in the tens of millions to people the burgeoning capitalist economy of the North even as the American peasants were kept to the margin. Here, it seems to me, is a clear implication of "racial dishonor" in early twentieth-century America. Few powerful people at the time desired to see millions of black Americans—their fellow citizens—moving out of the South, to the great northern cities. In the event, black migration to the Promised Land of urban opportunity lagged behind that of European ethnics by decades. And when black migrants finally began to arrive, and to compete for housing, jobs, and political power, they encountered fierce resistance from the relatively new Americans of that day.[7]

Contemporary public deliberations over policy issues like welfare and crime also provide evidence of racial stigma at work. Investigators studying the determinants of state-level welfare policy in the wake of the 1996 reform of federal welfare laws (giving states greater autonomy to set their regulations) are beginning to uncover evidence that jurisdictions with more blacks on the rolls have used their newfound discretion to implement more punitive revisions of their welfare regulations—being more likely to cap benefits to mothers who have additional children while on the rolls, to impose time limits and work requirements for beneficiaries stricter than the minimal federal requirement, and so on (Soss et al., 2001). Studies of the way the news media cover poverty and welfare issues tell a similar story. The political scientist Martin Gilens combed through all of the issues of three leading news magazines, *U.S. News and World Report*, *Time*, and *Newsweek*, published between 1950 and 1992, analyzing how photographs were used to depict the poor in the stories dealing with poverty and welfare (Gilens 1999). He found that over half of all poor people pictured were African American, even though on the average blacks made up less than one-third of the poor during this period. Most revealingly, though, he also found that the overrepresentation of blacks in these media-generated images of poverty was greatest when the general public mood was least sympathetic to the poor; that stories showing "problem cases" among welfare recipients used black images at a higher rate than could be accounted for by blacks' representation among such cases; and that, despite blacks' general overrepresentation in these images of the poor, whites were overrepresented in the pictures accompanying stories about "success cases."

The jails of America overflow with young black men. The number incarcerated on a given day has more than quadrupled over the past two decades, largely as a consequence of our anti-drug law enforcement policies (see Tonry 1995). Consider some of the ethical issues raised by our drug enforcement regime. Here we are, a rich nation with a segment of its middle class interested in consuming the very substances that another segment of its middle class is interested in outlawing. And so we carry on an illicit commerce to the tune of $100 billion a year, drawing coca out of the ground in Bolivia and Peru, through Colombian processing facilities and transshipment points farther north, corrupting everything in its wake: government officials in Mexico and the Caribbean as well as our own urban police departments. And yet when we decide to take action against this commerce we balance our cultural budget on the backs of the weakest and the darkest of our fellow citizens, though they are by no means the only users. That is a social fact that impresses me, and I see stigma, the nonattribution of a common humanity, at the core of that problem.

Why is there so little public debate in the United States about what is a really dramatic social fact? We now have nearly 1.2 million African Americans under lock and key. We have huge urban neighborhoods where the norm is that young men will spend time in jail, where the entire communal life orients around gray stone buildings—institutions dedicated to the physical control of human bodies. This is the Land of Liberty, yet some class/race-defined segments of the society literally live in a police state. Now, perhaps that must be so. But why is there no public reflection about it? Why does this circumstance not create dissonance? How is it that our moralists and our political leaders are able to sleep at night in the face of these facts?

Dramatic racial disparity in imprisonment rates does not occasion more public angst, I claim, because this circumstance does not strike the typical American observer at the cognitive level as being counterintuitive. It does not to a sufficient degree disappoint some deeply held, taken-for-granted expectations and assumptions about the nature of our society. It can be accounted for by a narrative line attributing the outcome to the inadequacies of the persons who suffer the condition, not to any as yet undiscovered problems with our own social organization.

The public's response to black/white differences in imprisonment rates is almost as muted as is its response to male/female differences. Regarding the latter, the public line, in effect, is this: "Everybody knows that men are more violent and aggressive than women, so the disparity comes as no surprise." This is not often said directly, but it is the tacit public belief, and it may be a valid claim about gender differences. Few thoughtful people would knowingly espouse such a view about racial disparity, however. Yet, given the vast overrepresentation of blacks among those held in state custody, the lack of any sense of alarm in American public discourses suggests that collective decisions about criminal justice policy are being taken, at least tacitly, as if such racial essentialism were a widely held view. That is, by failing to consider how our policies, in conjunction with racially influenced patterns of social interaction, may be generating an unfair outcome, we act in effect as though the problem here lies with THEM and not—as is, in fact, the case—with ALL OF US.

I maintain the following: If there were a comparable number of young European-American men on beer-drinking binges, or anorexic teenage girls starving themselves to death, and if these were situations in which the same degree of human suffering was engendered as is being produced in this case, it would occasion a most profound reflection about what had gone wrong, not only with THEM, but also with US. "What manner of people are we to produce such an outcome?" would become a key question. It would never be dismissed with the thought that those people are simply reaping what they have sown. It would disturb us at our core. So the question becomes, What disturbs us? What is dissonant? What seems anomalous? What is contrary to expectation? A racial group is stigmatized when it can experience an alarming disparity in some social indicators, and yet that disparity occasion no societal reflection upon the extent to which that circumstance signals something having gone awry in OUR structures rather than something having gone awry in THEIRS.

This example illustrates my point that important political results follow from the ways citizens process social information and the causal mechanisms they are prepared to credit. Will we, in the face of the astronomically high rates of black incarceration, consider modifying our institutional practices or not?

Here is another thought experiment: Consider two alternative anti-drug law enforcement regimes, broadly put. Regime 1 looks mainly to the selling side of the transactions, finding as many of those bad drug dealers as possible and locking them up for as long as possible. Regime 2 looks to the buying side of the transaction, but with the same intensity, leading to the same rate of incarceration of people caught in retail drug buys. Suppose that just as many prisons are to be built and just as severe a sentencing regime is to be installed under Regime 2. We are intent on locking up the buyers for just as long.

Notice that, when enforcement efforts concentrate on the buying side, those being held in the gray stone buildings, and those waiting on line to get past the metal detectors to visit them—the people receiving letters from loved ones who have been shut away, those weeping in vain for mercy before judges whose discretion has been taken away by mandatory sentencing laws—those people will be US. It is probable that we will perceive an anomaly here. Not only will our interests be more directly engaged. Our reading of the facts will be materially affected. We may thus be led to reconsider whether it is proper to impose such high costs on those relative few of our fellow citizens, so as to pursue a puritanical, hypocritical anti-drug law enforcement policy. Under Regime 1, in contrast, the punitive outcome for THEM may not be at all inconsistent with the narrative that many people embrace unreflectively about race-related matters in the United States: "We now have a growing black middle class. They play by the rules; they're doing just fine. These jokers out there on the corner, 'slinging rocks' and listening to 'gangsta rap,' need to be locked up. They are receiving their just deserts. They did the crime and so they are doing the time. After all, we must keep our cities' streets safe."

Now, that specific narrative has no objective, scientific warrant. It is not merely a reading of the evidence. It entails seeing facts through a particular interpretative lens. Social analysts should ask why this way of understanding reality seems compelling, despite the fact that we are loading tremendous costs onto some very vulnerable and disadvantaged people. Racial stigma is, I believe, a part of the answer. This, I am arguing here, is how deeply structured racial inequality in a society arises and persists over a long time.

The processes that engender it do not come under scrutiny or become the subject of public deliberations because too many observers are able to assimilate the relevant evidence into their "models" without questioning the underlying specification of the structures of social causation upon which they intuitively rely.

Consider the debate about race and intelligence that has raged in recent years thanks in large part to the bestselling book *The Bell Curve: Intelligence and Class Structure in American Life* (Herrnstein and Murray 1994). What does the typical well-educated American know about IQ differences among people from Tennessee, Texas, and Massachusetts? I venture that most Americans know next to nothing about such disparities, if any exist. What is more, I assert that it would be illegitimate to make a factual claim about such differences in a public argument over policy—to object to the interregional redistribution of resources, for example, on the grounds that people in the less advantaged regions are merely receiving their IQ-adjusted deserts. Or I can put the point somewhat differently. The American population is aging, and it is known that intelligence declines as a person ages, after some point in the life cycle. It is a demographic certainty that there will be relatively more older people in the American population in the years to come, and it is a legal fact that laws against age discrimination have abrogated mandatory retirement. These things taken together imply, as a mathematical necessity, that the American workforce is going to be made "dumber" by those baby boomers who insist on staying in the workforce beyond their prime years. Where can one read about the dire consequences of this development for the productivity of the American economy? Nowhere. Why not? The reason, I suggest, is that those older, soon-to-be-less-intelligent workers are our mothers and fathers. We are not about to set them to one side and engage in an elaborate discourse about their fitness. And if they are "dumb," then they are our "dumb" moms and dads. Like those living in different regions, we who belong to different generations will not permit ourselves to be sundered by any civic boundary. We will sink or swim together.

The point here, once again, is that some social disparities are salient and others not. The salience of social facts is not determined in an entirely rational, deductively confirmed manner. It involves a mode of cognition that depends on some prior patterning or orientation that is not, itself, the product of conscious reflection.

Permit me one further illustration. *American Enterprise* magazine is the public policy journal of the American Enterprise Institute, an influential right-of-center think tank in Washington, D.C. An editorial commentary in the magazine on the problem of racial inequality began by speaking of "a great disloyal and responsibility-free underclass culture" (disloyal!) from which "decent citizens of all races" have fled (Zinsmeister 1996, p. 4). (Of course, the comment goes on, decent people care about the plight of the underclass. But there are no external solutions to be had for their problems.)

"The troubling reality in our ghettos today is that the hellish torments are being inflicted by their own residents. If only some identifiable outside force were creating the siege conditions, nearly any American would gladly swing a battle-axe against such an enemy. But the harder, more tragic reality is that inner-city Americans are being brutalized by their own neighbors, their own reproductive partners, their own teenagers, their own mothers even. And ultimately, by themselves. Who is forcing the crack pipe between those many lips?" (p. 5). Here, then, we have a mainstream conservative policy institution directing its attention to inner-city poverty. And what do we see? The stark revelation of an US-THEM racial dichotomy embraced so instinctually and casually that the writer seems oblivious to it! Here we can clearly see racial stigma at work in America today.

It is important to attend to racial stigma in American political culture because, in general, people do not freely give the presumption of equal humanity. Only philosophers do that, and may God love them! But the rest of us tend to ration the extent to which we will presume an equal humanity of our fellows. One cannot necessarily count on getting the benefit of that presumption. So in an industrial society of nearly three hundred million people with a history going back centuries, what happens when tens of millions of those people cannot in every situation of moral reflection and significant public deliberation rely upon being extended the presumption of an equal humanity?

Again, I want to stress, "racism" is too coarse a category to do the analytical work that needs doing here. Exactly what is the nature of racism? What is its mechanism? *I want to suggest with the stigma idea that a withholding of the presumption of equal humanity is the ultimate mechanism of racism in American public life.* It will be hard to nail that one down by searching through government statistics for evidence of racial discrimination. The effects of stigma are surely more subtle than that. Those effects are deeply embedded in the symbolic and expressive life of the nation, and in the narrative account that is finally to be told about the nation's origins and destiny.

Thus we are often said to be a nation of immigrants. Thirty million newcomers have arrived on our shores since the liberalization of immigration laws in the 1960s. They have advanced up the escalator of opportunity, by and large. Now, what will the story be? Here is one possibility: "We are a great nation, an open society, the land of opportunity. True, there are millions of laggard blacks, and that's too bad. It is regrettable that we need to lock up one million of them on any given day. And it is too bad that some two out of five of these black children depend on a public welfare system that has just been reformed in such a manner that, absent a boom economy, they may suffer a great deal. True, we have of late engaged in a discourse about the intellectual inadequacies of these blacks—a discourse that leaves it an open question whether or not, or the extent to which, those inadequacies are rooted in the inherent incapacities of their genetic endowments. But, as best we can determine, no individual's rights are being violated when he or she applies for an employment or educational opportunity, and we intend to make sure this remains the case. True, some blacks are falling behind, but most of the recent immigrants are not of European origins either, and they are doing pretty well by and large. So as far as racial justice is concerned, America is okay."

Now, is that simply racism? Yes and no, I would say. Yes, it is racism, but by no means is it *simply* racism. How, the question becomes, will it be contested? What will the argument be? "Don't compare blacks to immigrants"? Frankly, my view is that analysts ought to be wary of such comparisons, but I do not see how they can be avoided. "Don't publish those test score data"? I seriously doubt that anyone is going to put the genie back in the bottle on that one either. But how about this: Adopt as an axiom from the outset a belief in the equal humanity of these sons and daughters of slaves. Make this an a priori commitment that is not contingent on any empirical determination. The view would be that they are equal humanly with us, and that we swim or sink together. This view would be taught to the new Americans at their first step off the boat. We would not allow them to cluster in Miami, thinking that they have made a wondrous new world on the shores of industrial capitalism and liberal democracy, while the laggards over in Liberty City riot every now and then, and otherwise suck on the welfare tit. Before they get the citizenship paper, we would make sure they know the story of the country—that is, the decent story, the narrative that has some chance of being sustained under appropriate moral scrutiny. A central aspect of that story is that one-quarter or so of the black American population languishes in the Liberty Cities of the nation because we have a public culture in which the presumption of their equal humanity has not yet been fully extended.

As things stand, our immigrants are learning a rather different lesson. In fact, one of the first things newcomers to America discover about their adopted country is that African Americans are a stigmatized group, to be avoided at all costs. The sociologist Camille Charles has provided some powerful evidence in support of this claim. In a recently published study (Charles 2000), she analyzed data from an intriguing survey designed to measure preferences among various ethnic groups in Los Angeles for the ethnic and racial composition of a respondent's ideal neighborhood. Subjects were shown a card with an array of empty boxes representing houses in a hypothetical residential area, and were asked to imagine their home being in the middle of this array. Then they were told to "imagine an ideal neighborhood that had the ethnic and racial mix you, personally, would feel most comfortable in" (p. 386). To describe this ideal neighborhood, they could write either "A" for Asian, "H" for Hispanic, "B" for Black, or "W" for White in the boxes on the card surrounding their imagined home. Charles found that 40 percent of Asians, 32 percent of Latinos, and 19 percent of whites envisioned their ideal neighborhood, in which they would feel most comfortable, as one containing no blacks. Tellingly, immigrants were much more averse to living near blacks than were the native born among Asians and Latinos. Native-born Latinos and Asians had rates of "Black exclusion" (no blacks in the ideal neighborhood) of 17 percent and 15 percent, respectively. This was comparable to the 19 percent rate for whites. But among the foreign-born, 37 percent of Latinos and 43 percent of Asians envisioned an "ideal neighborhood" as one that excluded blacks entirely.

BEYOND DISCRIMINATION

Recall Axiom 2, which constrains this theoretical project by a baseline presumption that I have called "anti-essentialism." Explaining protracted and durable racial inequality becomes relatively easy if one admits the possibility of inherent racial differences in human attributes that significantly influence the ability of individuals to act effectively (intelligence, for example). I reject this possibility a priori, and I do so for two reasons: It is impossible to prove that no such innate racial differences exist; one can only show this view to be more or less plausible. Not everyone will be persuaded. More to the point, however, in a raced polity committed to democratic values, a public discourse that imputes inherent incapacity to some raced group of citizens is fundamentally inconsistent with the espoused democratic ideals. Policy argument in such a political setting, I have been suggesting, should as a matter of civic duty proceed under the maintained hypothesis of anti-essentialism. (Such a posture inhibits vicious circles of cumulative causation detrimental to the stigmatized group from ever getting started.)

The anti-essentialist position amounts to the assertion that, just as race is a social convention, so too, any widespread, durable, large-scale racial group disparity in status is a socially constructed, not a natural, outcome. It follows from anti-essentialism that a successful and consistent theory of racial inequality will need to account for the relatively disadvantaged position of African Americans by reference to processes that block in a systematic way the realization of the human potential of the members of this racial group. One can do so, it would appear, in only two ways: One can show that the rewards accruing to the members of the disadvantaged group, given their productivity, are lower than the rewards garnered by others. Or one can show that, owing to processes unrelated to their innate capabilities, members of the disadvantaged racial group lack opportunity to realize their productive potential. (These means of argument can, of course, be used in combination; it need not be either one or the other.)

These, then, are two distinct modalities for my project, what I will call an exercise in "racial apologetics." (The term "apologetics" is borrowed from Christian theology, where a rough definition might be "defending the reasonableness of the faith." It is the reasonableness of my faith in the racial anti-essentialism postulate that I endeavor to defend here.) In the first mode of argument, one undertakes to show that, systematically, productivity is rewarded differently for members of distinct racial groups. Call this the reward bias argument. In the second mode, one shows that, systematically, opportunity to acquire productivity is unequally available to the members of distinct racial groups. Call this the development bias argument.[8] While I believe that both reward bias and development bias characterize the situation of African Americans in the United States, there is a profoundly significant distinction to be drawn between these two modes of argument for both the social-theoretic and the social-philosophic aspects of my analysis.

Another name for the reward bias argument is discrimination. There is an extensive literature in the social sciences and in social philosophy on the problem of racial discrimination. Yet I am not enthusiastic about this concept; I argue here that it should be demoted, dislodged from its current prominent place in the conceptual discourse on racial inequality in American life. Instead, I believe that the concept of racial stigma should have a more prominent place in this discourse. This belief rests on my conviction that racial discrimination, as an analytical category, cannot reach the problem of development bias. It is useful mainly in the context of argumentation about reward bias. And yet I see the development bias argument as the more promising one for my racial apologetics project, for two reasons. In the first place, it explains the extent and durability of current racial inequality more effectively. But more important, the dilemmas of public morality created by racial inequality in the United States, given the nation's history and the unique place of blacks within it, can be fully illuminated only when the development bias problem is placed at center stage.

Most discussion of the topic of race and social justice in the United States, whether in the social sciences or in social philosophy, has been centered on the concept of discrimination. As an historical practice, this is appropriate and understandable. It was, after all, animus against racial discrimination that prompted those monumental achievements—the Supreme Court's 1954 *Brown* decision and the Civil Rights Act of 1964—which ultimately established equality of citizenship for the descendants of slaves as a matter of law in the United States. The legal apparatus erected on this foundation endeavors to enforce equality of treatment of individuals in public and quasi-public spaces—the public schools, the labor market, the voting booth. This history, and the palpable fact of overt racial bias in employment, housing, government services, and the larger American cultural life, well into the middle of the twentieth century, explains why discrimination became a classic way of stating the problem of race-based social injustice.

But things have changed a great deal since the 1950s. Racial discrimination in the public sphere is a relatively straightforward, universally recognized moral problem. Almost everyone now agrees that such discrimination should be proscribed in the interest of creating a "level playing field." (Of course, there is plenty of disagreement over just how this should be done.) But entrenched racial disparity in developmental opportunities is an intractable, often neglected moral problem—one that (as I will argue momentarily) gives rise to unavoidable conflicts between cherished values and challenges settled intuitions about social justice.

So for both empirical and philosophical reasons I conclude that a continued focus on the classic racial discrimination problem is now misplaced: Anti-black reward bias has declined sharply in the United States over the past half-century. And the normative challenge posed by enduring racial inequality can be fully grasped and effectively met only if greater attention is given to the problem of development bias.

TWO KINDS OF DISCRIMINATION

To see this more clearly, let us consider an elemental distinction between two kinds of behavior: discrimination in contract and discrimination in contact. The phrase "discrimination in contract" is meant to invoke the unequal treatment of otherwise like persons on the basis of race in the execution of formal transactions—the buying and selling of goods and services, for instance, or interactions with organized bureaucracies, public and private. Discrimination in contract, in other words, is a standard means by which reward bias against blacks has been effected. By contrast, "discrimination in contact" refers to the unequal treatment of persons on the basis of race in the associations and relationships that are formed among individuals in social life, including the choice of social intimates, neighbors, friends, heroes, and villains. It involves discrimination in the informal, private spheres of life.[9]

Now, there is a fundamental difference between these types of discrimination. Discrimination in contract occurs in settings over which a liberal state could, if it were to choose to do so, exercise review and restraint in pursuit of social justice (subject, of course, to the limitations of information and authority that inhibit any regulatory enterprise). Thus, and thankfully, the U.S. courts no longer enforce racially restrictive covenants in real estate deeds, or allow employers to advertise that "no blacks need apply." Such discrimination is legally proscribed—a proscription seen not only as consistent with, but as necessary for, the realization of liberal ideals.

However, in any recognizably liberal political order some forms of discrimination in contact must remain a prerogative for autonomous individuals. Preserving the freedom of persons to practice this discrimination is essential to the maintenance of liberty for two reasons: The social exchanges from which such discrimination arises are so profoundly intimate and cut so close to the core of our being that all but the most modest interventions in this sphere must be avoided if liberty and autonomy are to have any real meaning. More fundamentally, while the ethical case against racial discrimination in formal (for example, market) transactions is relatively easy to make, it is far less obvious that there is anything wrong in principle with forming or avoiding close association with another person partly on the basis of racial identity.

Indeed, and ironically, it is probably true that effective resistance to racial domination requires that the black victims of that domination organize and motivate themselves to collective action through the systematic practice of problack discrimination in contact. That is, as a political (not a moral) proposition, practicing discrimination in contact may be essential to ending discrimination in contract. Moreover, to reverse the effects of generations of brutal, violent, humanity-denying racial oppression—effects manifested in the bodies, minds, and spirits of the victims of that oppression—it may be necessary to mount communal self-help efforts that can only succeed if the victims practice the selective racial associations that characterize discrimination in contact.

Both these claims—regarding collective action on behalf of the political and the communal revitalization objectives—are speculative, the second particularly so. But both are sufficiently plausible to illustrate why even the most dyed-in-the-wool integrationist ought to reject a blanket prohibition on discrimination in contact, and why a liberal individualist of any sophistication ought to reject that brittle, two-step liberalism that enshrines some mythical "unencumbered self"—a "self" located outside the flow of history and the web of culture—as a touchstone of moral judgment in regard to questions of racial pride, kinship, and fealty.

Given that individuals socialized in the United States understand themselves partly in racial terms, and that they must in any liberal political order be endowed with autonomy regarding the choice of their most intimate associations, it is inevitable that the selective patterns of social intercourse that are the stuff of discrimination in contact will arise.

So we have on the one hand a formal sector of contract and on the other hand what I refer to as the informal sector of contact. When discrimination in contract takes place, the tendency is to say that individuals are being treated unfairly and not being given their due. They are blatant victims of reward bias; they ought to be given their just reward. But, when discrimination in contact occurs, it is likely to be seen as a necessary if not always desirable consequence of our commitment to liberal principles. And, as I have been suggesting just now, when blacks practice this discrimination in defense of their own humanity, there may be no reason to find it in the least bit undesirable, let alone immoral.

In making this last observation I do not mean to suggest that any attempt to promote racial solidarity among blacks can be justified in this way. I merely maintain that internal institution building, mutual affirmation, and selective association are among the practices to be found in the collective mobilization toolkit on which an historically oppressed, racially stigmatized population must draw. To outsiders, such practices will look to be racially discriminatory—

because they are! Even so, insiders well may see the very same practices as being necessary, politically and existentially necessary—because, in fact, they are! From this observation I draw the modest conclusion that one is unlikely to find a single moral principle upon which to ground all judgments about the propriety of these two kinds of discrimination.

DISCRIMINATORY ASSOCIATIONS AND DEVELOPMENT BIAS

But, while discrimination in contact may not be as unambiguously objectionable on moral grounds as is discrimination in contract, its real-world consequences can be just as debilitating for a racially stigmatized group. This is because the mechanisms of social mobility and intergenerational status transmission operative within any society are crucially sensitive to the patterns of contact, as well as the rules of contract, at work in that society. Indeed, in the United States as elsewhere around the world, both formal and informal social relations mediate the provision of nearly all of the resources thought to be necessary for human development. As such, ending discrimination in contract can never ensure equality of developmental opportunity.

My argument here relies on the vast body of empirical work in the social sciences that has been devoted to establishing the central place of race in the relational structures that mediate social life in the United States. I have in mind here the roles played in the shaping of persons by the family, the social network, and (using the word advisedly) the "community." I am thinking about infant and early childhood development, and about adolescent peer-group influences. I mean to provoke some reflection on how people come to hold the ideas they, in fact, do hold concerning who they are (their identities), which other persons are essentially like them (their social identifications), and what goals in life are worth striving toward (their ideals). The fundamental empirical claim, taken here to have important philosophic implications upon which I will expand in the next chapter, is this: *In American society, where of historical necessity patterns of social intercourse are structured by perceptions of race, it is inevitable that developmental processes operating at the individual level will also be conditioned by race. Historic racial reward bias, combined with race-mediated social relations, can lead to current and future development bias, particularly if the racially marked population subgroup is stigmatized.*

Now, it should be possible to see why I hold that thinking in terms of discrimination, which is to say, loading most of the weight in the racial apologetics argument onto the case for reward bias, should be questioned. Empirical work on racial inequality by social scientists focuses almost entirely on the differential treatment of individuals, on the basis of race, in formal market transactions (jobs, housing, credit, and so on). Less attention is paid to underlying social processes that lead to racial differences in the acquisition of productive skills. The primary normative claim in this approach is that reward bias is a moral offense, a legitimate object of regulatory intervention, and a significant contributor to the scourge of racial inequality. I think these claims are all true. But implicit here also is the notion that, insofar as racial inequality is due to development bias—reflected in a disparity of skills presented to employers by black and white employees—similar moral issues are not raised, nor is comparable warrant given for intervention. I think this normative implication of the focus on reward bias is simply false.

It is becoming increasingly obvious in the United States that eliminating discrimination in markets cannot be expected to lead, even in the long term, to a solution for the problem of racial economic inequality. Like any good anti-essentialist, I hold that the substantial gap in skills between blacks and whites is itself the result of processes of social exclusion (discrimination in contact) that deserve to be singled out for explicit study and, where possible, for policy remedy. The inner workings of development bias should be explored more fully, with the role of racial stigma in these opportunity-blocking processes made more explicit.

This perspective does not come naturally to an economist. It is conventional in our discipline to posit an atomized agent acting more or less independently, seeking to make the best of opportunities at hand. For some time now I have been convinced that this way of thinking cannot adequately capture the ways that racial inequality persists over time. In actuality, individuals are embedded in complex networks of affiliations: They are members of nuclear and extended families; they belong to religious and linguistic groupings; they have ethnic and racial identities; they are attached to particular localities. Each individual is socially situated, and one's location within the network of social affiliations substantially affects one's access to various resources. Opportunity travels along the synapses of these social networks. Thus a newborn is severely handicapped if its parents are relatively uninterested in (or incapable of) fostering the youngster's intellectual development in the first years of life. A talented adolescent whose social peer group disdains the activities that must be undertaken for that talent to flourish is at risk of not achieving his or her full potential. An unemployed person without friends or relatives already at work in a certain industry may never hear about the job opportunities available there. An individual's inherited social situation plays a major role in determining his or her ultimate economic success.

In earlier work, I introduced the term "social capital" to suggest a modification of the standard human capital theory in economics. My modification was intended to provide a richer context within which to analyze racial inequality (Loury 1976, 1977). I formalized the observation that family and community backgrounds can play an important role, alongside factors like individual ability and human capital investments, in determining individual achievement. Some important part of racial inequality, on this view, arises from the way geographic and social segregation along racial lines, fostered by the stigmatized status of blacks—their "social otherness"—inhibits the development of their full human potential. Because access to developmental resources is mediated through race-segregated social networks, an individual's opportunities to acquire skills depend on present and past skill attainments by others in the same racial group.

STIGMA, DEVELOPMENT BIAS, AND RACIAL JUSTICE

This analysis has a crucial ethical implication: If a skilled workforce can be created only as a result of interactive social processes, then the celebration of meritocracy should be tempered with an understanding that no one travels the road to success alone. The fact is that generations overlap, much of social life takes place outside the reach of public regulation, and extant social affiliations condition the development of personal and intellectual skills in the young. As a result, present inequality—among individuals and between groups—must embody to some degree the social and economic disparities that have existed in the past. *If the past disparities are morally illegitimate, the propriety of the contemporary order must also be called into question.* I maintain that a theory of justice meant to apply to a racially hierarchical society such as the United States that fails to recognize this moral implication is unworthy of the name.

A moral analyst of any sophistication ought to recognize that societies are not amalgams of unrelated individuals creating themselves anew—out of whole cloth, as it were—in each generation. A complex web of social connections and a long train of historical influences interact to form the opportunities and shape the outlooks of individuals. Contracts are ubiquitous, true enough. But everything of importance in social life has an informal dimension. The effort, talent, and luck of an individual are crucial, of course. But what a person achieves also results from the social background, cultural affinities, and communal associations to which he or she is heir.

Hence, while there may be a grain of truth in the insistence by conservatives that cultural differences lie at the root of racial disparity in the United States, the deeper truth is that, for some three centuries now, political, social, and economic institutions that by any measure must be seen as racially oppressive have distorted the communal experience of the slaves and their descendants. When we look at stigmatized "underclass culture" in American cities of today we are seeing a product of that oppressive history, perpetuated now via discrimination in contact, and engendering profound development bias.

Thinking in this way, I believe, helps account for the durable racial inequality with which America is still encumbered. Consider the so-called black underclass—the poor central-city dwellers who make up perhaps a quarter of the

African-American population. In the face of the despair, violence, and self-destructive folly of so many of these people, it is morally superficial in the extreme to argue as many conservatives now do that "if those people would just get their acts together, like many of the poor immigrants, we would not have such a horrific problem in our cities." To the contrary, any morally astute response to the "social pathology" of American history's losers would conclude that, while we cannot change our ignoble past, we need not and must not be indifferent to the contemporary suffering issuing directly from that past, for which we bear some collective responsibility. (As a colleague of mine puts it, "Last guys don't finish nice!")

The "conservative line" on race in America today is simplistic. I repeat: The self-limiting patterns of behavior among poor blacks are not a product of some alien cultural imposition on a pristine Euro-American canvas. Rather, such "pathological" behavior by these most marginal of Americans is deeply rooted in American history. It evolved in tandem with American political and economic institutions, and with cultural practices that supported and legitimated those institutions—practices that were often deeply biased against blacks. So, while we should not ignore the behavioral problems of this so-called underclass, we should discuss and react to them as if we were talking about our own children, neighbors, and friends. This is an American tragedy. It is a national, not merely a communal disgrace.

And we should respond to it as we might to an epidemic of teen suicide or a run of high school shooting sprees—by embracing, not demonizing, the perpetrators, who, often enough, are also among the victims.

The conservative line on race is also ahistorical. Contemporary American society has inherited a racial hierarchy—the remnant of a system of racial domination that had been supported by an array of symbols and meanings deleterious to the reputation and self-image of blacks. It can be no surprise in such a society that the web of interconnections among persons that facilitate access to opportunity and shape the outlooks of individuals would be raced, which is to say, that processes of human development would be systematically conditioned by race.

Thus, racially disparate outcomes at the end of the twentieth century can be no surprise, either. The "comparative narrative"—"structural reform is not needed; blacks may be lagging but nonwhite immigrants are progressing nicely, so America must be okay"—is sophomoric social ethics and naïve social science. Saying this in no way commits me to the view that success is independent of effort, or that victims of racism should be exempted from mandates of personal responsibility.

The problem with stigmatizing talk about "black culture," "black crime," and "black illegitimacy"—when used as explanatory categories by the morally obtuse—is that such talk becomes an exculpatory device, a way of avoiding a discussion of mutual obligation. A distressing fact about contemporary American politics is that simply to make this point is to risk being dismissed as an apologist for the inexcusably immoral behavior of the poor. In truth, the moral failing here lies with those who would wash their hands of the poor, declaring "we've done all we can." And it is to an analysis of this moral failing that I now turn.

4

RACIAL JUSTICE

IT WILL be helpful to summarize the argument to this point. I have argued that race is best thought of as a social convention: Markings on the bodies of human beings—of no intrinsic significance in themselves—become invested through time with reasonable expectations and powerful social meanings. Seeing race as a conventional, not a natural, category suggests that no innate, sizable disparity of human potential between distinct racial groups exists. So no appeal to innate racial difference can explain African-American disadvantage. Yet because race conventions can seem to be natural and quite consistent with reason, and because they convey significant social meanings, people with particular race-markers may become stigmatized—seen by their fellows as "damaged goods," as THEM not US, as persons who lack the ability or "culture" to succeed in society's mainstream. Moreover, since legitimate public action in a democracy must comport with how observers interpret social experience, and because the meanings connected with race conventions can distort social-cognitive processes in the citizenry to the detriment of the stigmatized, reform policies that ameliorate the disadvantage of the racial "other" may fail to garner a majority's support. I argued in Chapter 3 that black Americans are a stigmatized people in this sense. I want now to investigate what might be implied by this view for the pursuit of social justice in the United States.

Two distinct moral desiderata animate the discourse about race and social justice in America. One view I will call "race-blindness"—the conviction that racial identity should play no part in the way people are treated in public life, that we should be "blind" to race. The other view I will call "race-egalitarianism"—the conviction that, because of an unjust history, we should endeavor to reduce inequalities of wealth and power between racial groups, as such. It is instructive to contrast these two ideas. Race-blindness is a procedural standard. It deals with prerogatives of the individual. It emphasizes autonomy and impartiality. And it does not depend on history—either for its rationale or for its implementation. Advocacy of "blindness" in this sense, as a touchstone of moral public action in matters of race, is a natural consequence of a commitment to liberal individualism.

By contrast, race-egalitarianism focuses explicitly on the status of groups. It entails looking not only at the procedures employed in a society but also at the social outcomes those procedures generate. And it finds its justification in a comprehensive understanding of how current racial disparities have come to be. Thus race-egalitarianism is a view that conflicts to a degree with the precepts of liberal individualism.

I will be arguing here for a priority of these moral concerns: race-egalitarianism over race-blindness. My view is that one cannot think sensibly about social justice issues in a racially divided society if one does not attend to the race-mediated patterns of social intercourse that characterize interpersonal relations in that society. Once the reality of these racially biased interactive patterns is taken into account, race-blindness begins to look much less attractive as a moral position, precisely because of its individualistic, ahistorical, and purely procedural focus.

ANONYMITY AND LIBERAL NEUTRALITY

To aid in the development of this argument, I invite the reader to consider the formidable intellectual edifice that is modern social choice theory. This literature at the junction of economics and philosophy pursues the formal, logical derivation of implications for public decision-making that issue from various postulates chosen to capture ethical intuitions about social justice. Over the last half-century, social choice theory has been central to the ambition of laying down a coherent intellectual foundation for the normative assessment of public action. Its best-known text is also its founding text: Kenneth Arrow's monumental *Social Choice and Individual Values* (Arrow 1963). The reputation in philosophy and economics of another Nobel Laureate, Amartya Sen, is also grounded on his early work in this field.

A question of fundamental importance is raised in this literature—a question concerning the right ordering of relations between the state (which has a monopoly on the legitimate exercise of coercion) and the citizenry (which must live with the consequences of state action). That question may be posed as follows: Suppose some social, public, or collective choice is to be made, and that individuals can rank the alternatives from among which that choice will be taken. Individuals are capable, that is, of putting the alternatives into an order—of saying, from their personal points of view, which is the most desirable, second most, third most, and so forth. Further, imagine that—in an expression of collective rationality—this public choice, the one to be enforced by the state, is to be taken in accordance with some (now) collective or public ranking scheme. Then how ought this collective ordering of social alternatives to relate to the rankings of individuals?

Surely, in a society that values liberty (may I and my children ever live in such a place!), there must be some link between these two. The state's actions, imposed by force on all of us, ought to "respect" in some way our individual valuations. So the central question of social choice theory is whether and how the evaluative criterion guiding public decisions with collective consequences can be derived from the evaluative criteria held by individual citizens. The relationship between the values of individuals and the criterion of social choice cannot be arbitrary—else "liberty" is a sham.

Do not misunderstand. I am not here celebrating freedom to the exclusion of all other values. Nor do I claim that the only dimension of freedom worthy of consideration finds its expression in the linkage between individuals' preferences and the criteria of public choice. Still, if collective choices among public policies—between preserving the environment and "growing" the economy, for instance—are made in a manner that is neither responsive to nor reflective of the "will(s) of the people," then surely the persons living in that society do not enjoy a degree of autonomy that most of us would associate with freedom. So social choice theory expresses, in a formal and logically precise way, one of the central problems of liberal political theory.

Now, I invoke this theory so as to sharpen my discussion of the question at hand: How ought we Americans approach the public issue of pronounced and durable racial inequality? I believe that liberal theory is inherently limited in its capacity to engage this question, and a consideration of the social choice problem helps us to see why. An oft-imposed constraint on the relationship between individual and collective valuation in the social choice literature is the so-called Anonymity Axiom. This is a postulate that declares it to be illegitimate for the social ranking to favor one state of affairs over another—A over B, say—if the only distinction between the two situations is that the identities of persons located in various positions of the social order have been changed. That is, let situations A and B entail the same number of persons in poverty, with inadequate health care, held in prison, and the like, but with different groups of people suffering these conditions in situations A and B. "Anonymity" in public choice requires that state action express no preference between these two situations.

This is a kind of neutrality. If the only reason to prefer one situation to another is that different people enjoy what is worth having or suffer what must be endured—then identity pure and simple will have been allowed to dictate public valuation. This, a certain brand of liberal social philosophy holds, amounts to giving some people power over others on the basis of nothing more substantial than who they happen to be. The "anonymity" postulate rules such an eventuality out of bounds.

Notice one thing, however. An immediate corollary of this axiom is that a project to reduce inequality between identity-based groups in society—for its own sake, and not merely as a means to some other, identity-neutral end—would have to be judged an illegitimate social goal. This is because pursuing racial equality for its own sake means valuing more highly a situation in which racial disparities are reduced, even if overall inequality among persons remains unchanged. Ultimately, my argument in this chapter rejects this implication of "anonymity" as a requirement of social choice. Thus, perforce, I must argue against the axiom itself. Race-blindness, when interpreted so as to delegitimate actions needed to foster greater racial equality in contemporary American public life, is one expression of the liberal neutrality principle underlying the Anonymity Axiom. I will argue here that race-blindness represents a superficial moral stance, given the historical situation, and that it should be rejected.

More generally, I call into question the adequacy of liberal individualism as a normative theory, given the historical fact of racial subordination and the continuing reality of racial inequality. I suggest that there are questions of social ethics arising under these conditions—in societies sharply stratified along racial lines—to which liberal individualism gives no good answers.

By "liberal individualism" I refer to the tendency of thought that seeks to critically assess the justice of a society's distribution of resources solely in terms of the welfare of individuals, while giving no independent weight to the economic or social position of identity-based groups. I think this tendency of thought particular to liberalism is mistaken. I think (and think I can show) that it is an error to see only individuals, and never groups, as the legitimate subjects of a discourse on social equity. I believe (and believe I can demonstrate) that the manner in which liberal political theory deals with the ethical problems raised by the pronounced and durable social-economic disadvantage of African Americans is troubled, inadequate, superficial, and incomplete.

My topic, then, is racial justice. Now, as just suggested, it is impossible to avoid a philosopher's quibble over this use of words. Taking "racial" as modifier of "justice" inevitably raises hackles, because doing so declares an interest in the well-being of groups of persons—groups defined in terms of something called "race." Liberals fear that the freedom, dignity, integrity, autonomy, and/or rights of individuals will be trodden underfoot in a mad rush to obtain justice for fictitious "races." Beneath the surface of ostensibly progressive rhetoric about "racial justice," liberal individualists detect the distinct odor of an unjustifiable essentialism—a retrograde belief in racial essences.

I disagree. The concerns expressed by liberal critics of the idea of "racial justice," though not unreasonable, are nevertheless misplaced. Indeed, I hold that public talk about justice for racial groups is necessary for an intellectually rigorous and historically relevant social criticism in the United States. Moreover, I think it possible to conceive of social justice in regard to matters of race in such a way that the pitfalls liberals most fear can be avoided.

WHY USE "WHITE PHILOSOPHY"?

Some readers may wonder why I have chosen this way of framing the discussion in the first place. Is it not obvious, a critic might ask, that the liberalism of the European Enlightenment will be inadequate to the task of defining and pursuing racial justice? Why, that is, would I be content to work within what the philosopher Charles Mills calls "white philosophy,"[1] given that no less a figure than Immanuel Kant held racist anthropological views, that John Locke profited from slave trading, or that Thomas Jefferson fathered the children of Sally Hemmings? Why, this hypothetical critic might go on, would I even bother to criticize a purportedly trans-racial ethical tradition that served merely to cover European domination of nonwhite bodies? Here were theoretic reflections supposedly of universal significance that advanced hand-in-glove with the European appropriation of the world.

The tension here between ideal and practice is substantial, and Mills exploits it—not just rhetorically. Mills has interesting things to say about epistemology, for example, about how whites in the name of trans-racial ideals can be conveniently blind to the reality of the raced cultural and political spaces from which they benefit. They can refuse to see certain things—being not colorblind, but just blind. Mills can be quite interesting, and his argument with "white philosophy" is often pertinent to my concerns here. His essay on Frederick Douglass's "Whose Fourth of July?" is a marvelous illustration of this point (Mills 1998, ch. 8). At bottom, Mills argues there that Frederick Douglass stood in 1852 and gave a July 4th address that idealized the Founders' conception of universality, in contrast to the conception held by the ruling white elite of America circa 1852, an elite that continued to tolerate the institution of slavery. Whose Fourth of July, Douglass asked. Evidently it is not that of "our" Founding Fathers. (Linger, if you will, on the exquisitely ambiguous antecedent for that first person pronoun!)

Mills argues, persuasively in my view, that Douglass's historical reconstruction was fanciful. He claims that Roger Taney's now notorious opinion in the *Dred Scott* case (that blacks have no rights that a white need respect) was by far the more accurate account of prevailing opinion at the time of the Founding. He observes further that, by crediting the Founders as moral exemplars and exhorting his contemporaries to return to that state of virtue, Douglass had just written the Native Americans out of the domain of American social justice. All of that seems right. It seems right to say that, with few exceptions, the Founders thought the Africans in their midst were not quite fully human. They did not see them—my ancestors (well, some of my ancestors, anyway!)—as part of the social contract. No, they didn't put the word "slavery" in the Constitution—true enough. They merely put the institution of slavery under the protection of the Constitution—rather a worse offense.

But here is the problem, and the source of my dissatisfaction with Mills's argument, and the reason I am not, just now, hunting for what the social critic Cornel West has called a "counter-hegemonic political theory": What are we to do? Overthrow Kantian ethics? And put what, exactly, in its place? Do we think democratic ideas are bad ideas? Do we think that striving for a racially transcendent, non-particularistic understanding of how we should interact with one another is an unworthy quest? To recognize the flaws of the liberal tradition is one thing; to replace it with something workable is quite another. How are we going to govern ourselves? Are we to cherish representative institutions—and the rule of law? These are all the fruit of the Enlightenment, these ideas. One cannot throw them off because some of the Founding Fathers were themselves duplicitous or hypocritical. Thus a historically oriented effort to expose the particularity at the core of universalistic arguments may be interesting, but it is not a refutation of the universalistic claims.

So, with due humility, I am a reformer, not an "abolitionist," when it comes to political liberalism. But I object to the sociological naiveté, and the limited attention to history, which I think must be associated with liberal theory as applied to the problem of racial inequality.

THE TROUBLE WITH LIBERALISM

Succinctly stated, my problem with liberal individualism is that it fails to comprehend how stigma-influenced dynamics in the spheres of social interaction and self-image production can induce objective racial inequality, decoupled from contemporaneous discriminatory acts of individuals, carrying over across generations, shaping political and social-cognitive sensibilities in the citizenry, making racial disparity appear natural and nondissonant, stymieing reform, and locking in inequality.[2] The core point for me is that those "selves" who are the enshrined subjects of liberal theory—the autonomous, dignity-bearing individuals whose infinite value (ends in themselves, never means to an end) has been enshrined by Immanuel Kant at the center of the liberal project—these selves are not given a priori. They are, instead, products of social relations, and of economic and political institutions. That is, the selves at the center of liberal theory are, to a not inconsiderable degree, creatures of the very systems of laws, social intercourse, and economic relations that a normative theory is to assess.[3] Neither their goals in life nor (crucial for my purposes here) their self-understandings as raced subjects come into being outside the flow of history and the web of culture.

And so the diminished selves, the self-doubting, alienated, nihilistic, self-destructive selves—these are social products. I want to attend to this fact within the project of political theory. I cannot abide the imposition of abstract strictures of neutrality upon a game in which systematically nonneutral practices have left so many raced and stigmatized outsiders with so few good cards to play.

I reiterate: This is not some over-theorized discourse in defense of affirmative action policies. I desperately want to avoid having the far-reaching implications of my argument projected onto the narrow and partisan ground of the debate over racial preferences. I am not motivated here by a desire to preserve special treatment for blacks, or to keep someone's child from being admitted to a prestigious college. Rather, I am moved by the specter of one million African-American men physically confined in penal institutions, by the fact that the average black seventeen-year-old reads with the proficiency of the average white thirteen-year-old, and by the racial poverty rates, unemployment rates, and marriage patterns that are documented in the Appendix. The position I hold is that race is not irrelevant to these problems. One ought not to be "colorblind" when addressing them. Race is important not only for technical reasons, or instrumentally—these being problems whose solutions might entail race-conscious action. Race also matters in American society, in regard to problems of this kind, because these disparities rest upon and in turn serve to reinforce powerful social meanings detrimental to blacks.

Moreover, I believe that the phenomenon of racial stigma poses intractable problems for liberal individualism. For there is a sphere of intimate social intercourse, governed to some degree by raced perceptions in individuals' minds, that, out of respect for liberty and the dignity of human beings, should not become the object of political or bureaucratic manipulation. Yet, as I have argued, race-preferential associative behavior helps perpetuate a regime of development bias against blacks, largely because of a protracted, ignoble history during which reward bias against blacks was the norm. How, then, can racial justice be achieved while individual autonomy is respected? Thinking in terms of racial stigma provides insight into race-constrained social interactions, and into race-influenced processes of social cognition, exposing the forces at work in a raced society like the United States that create causal feedback loops perpetuating racial inequality, and that impede their identification. Moreover, this way of looking at things leads me to reject colorblindness (or the related notions of race-neutrality and racial impartiality) as *the* moral standard in regard to issues of social justice and racial inequality in the United States.

True, the so-called underclass in the ghettos of America is behaving badly, in self-destructive and threatening ways. But those patterns of behavior, embodied in those individuals, reflect structures of human development that are biased because of a history of deprivation and racial oppression. The result then is to produce, in our time, wide disparities in some indicia of behavior across racial groups. What does the abstract individualism of liberal theory suggest that we do now? Throw up our hands? Declare that no questions of justice are raised? Scratch our heads and say that we don't quite know what to do? Too bad, we lament, but . . . There is, I believe, a gaping hole in any normative framework that can provide us with no better answers than those.

HISTORICAL CAUSATION AND SOCIAL JUSTICE

I have been invoking history as a factor conditioning the ethical assessment of contemporary social arrangements. And yet the explicit channels of historical influence, on which social scientific work can shed some light, must of necessity remain opaque and vaguely specified. What might be called an "epistemological fog" obscures the causal dynamics at work across the generations and limits our ability to know in detail how past events have shaped current arrangements. Thus it may be reasonable to assert in a general way that past racial discrimination in contract, together with present discrimination in contact, disadvantages blacks by impeding their acquisition of skills. But it is nearly impossible to say with any quantitative precision just *how much* of current racial inequality is due to this source of disadvantage.

Consider the recent argument of Orlando Patterson on behalf of the proposition that the high rate of paternal abandonment of children among present-day African Americans is due to the devastating consequences for gender relations among blacks of American slavery, and of the racist system of Jim Crow segregation that followed (Patterson 1998). In my view, Patterson's argument is persuasive. But even so he can provide no answer to this crucial counterfactual query: What would family patterns be like among today's blacks in the absence of these historical depredations? This question is important because, without some sense of the extent of damage caused by past violation, it is difficult to gauge the appropriate scope of remedy.

Now, one could take the view, as some conservatives have done, that this limitation in knowledge should short-circuit claims for racial egalitarianism that rely upon the past unjust treatment of some racial group.[4] While acknowledging the plausibility of this view, I nevertheless reject it. Rather, I hold that a compensatory model, familiar from tort and liability law, is the wrong way to think about this question. My position, contrary to what I believe are simplistic applications of liberal neutrality that issue in mandates of colorblindness, is that *past racial injustice is relevant in establishing a general presumption against indifference to present racial inequality* (thereby militating against the implication of the Anonymity Axiom). But the degree to which social policy should be oriented toward reducing present racial inequality, the weight to be placed on this objective in the social decision calculus, is not here conceived in terms of "correcting" or "balancing" for historical violation. Thus I argue that, even though quantitative attribution of causal weight to distant historical events may not be possible, one can still support qualitative claims.

Indeed, a sharp contrast can be drawn between two categorically different responses to the problem of a morally problematic racial history. One seeks "reparations," conceiving the problem in *compensatory* terms. The other conceives the problem, let us say, in *interpretative* terms—seeking public recognition of the severity, and (crucially) the contemporary relevance, of what transpired. In the latter view, the goal is to establish a common baseline of historical memory—a common narrative, if you like—through which the past injury and its continuing significance can enter into current policy discourse. (A crude analogy might be drawn here, suggested by the debate over the Truth and Reconciliation Commission in post-Apartheid South Africa: The compensatory approach is rather like putting as many past offenders as possible on trial, punishing them for their wrongdoing, and getting justice for survivors of the victims. The interpretative approach is a bit like waiving the pursuit of individual criminal liability so as to shed public light on the true nature of what took place under Apartheid.) What seems conceptually important, though, is to clarify that, while some reckoning with the racist history of the United States remains to be done, this reckoning may, for political as well as epistemological reasons, be inappropriately cast in terms of "reparations." What is required, instead, is a commitment on the part of the public, the political elite, the opinion-shaping media, and so on to take responsibility for such situations as the contemporary plight of the urban black poor, and to understand them in a general way as a consequence of an ethically indefensible past. (This is not so much to "compensate" for an ethnically troubled past as to adopt the "right interpretation" of it.) Such a commitment would, on this view, be open-ended and not contingent on demonstrating any specific lines of causality.

This distinction between quantitative and qualitative historically based claims is also important, I think, because it casts doubt on the adequacy of purely procedural theories of justice in matters of race. Race-blindness is one such theory. In general, procedural theories of social justice turn on the answers to two kinds of questions: What are people entitled to? And what actions affecting the distribution of claims are legitimate? Then any state of affairs that respects individuals' entitlements and comes about from procedurally legitimate actions is held to be just. However, procedural theories are essentially incomplete, because they cannot cope with the consequences of their own violations.

Suppose we are given a set of rules about how people are to treat one another. Suppose further that people happen not always to follow these rules. As just noted, history can be messy stuff. Teasing out causal implications across the centuries of procedural violations is impossibly difficult. So if procedurally just requirements are not adhered to at some point—people entitled to the fruits of their labor are not rewarded accordingly, say—then at some later point, perhaps a century on, consequences will be rife in the interstices of society. But, as argued earlier, it will be impossible in principle to identify and to quantify these effects. What then would a procedural account have to say about this? Simple notions about providing compensation for identifiable historical wrongs may work when individual interactions are being considered, but they cannot possibly work for broad social violations—chattel slavery, for instance. A procedural theory leaves us with no account of justice under such circumstances. This is a fundamental incompleteness in the theory, one that is especially pertinent to a consideration of racial justice in the United States.[5]

To pursue this point somewhat more formally, let us call a system of rules about social justice *procedural* if it satisfies the following: (1) a list of rules or procedures is specified about how people are supposed to deal with one another; and (2) a state of affairs is held to be just if it evolves from a just original state, where every step in the evolution is brought about by the freely chosen actions of mutually consenting agents, all of which are consistent with the rules specified in (1). Furthermore, call such a system *closed to moral deviation* if it meets the following test: Whenever some state of affairs is brought about through actions by some agents that breach the rules specified in (1), it is in principle possible to "recover" from the effects of this breach through a series of counter-actions that are themselves consistent with the rules set out in (1).

In other words, a *procedural* account of social justice is *closed to moral deviation* if one can correct the consequences of rule violation through actions that are themselves consistent with the rules. In the absence of this "closure" property, a procedural theory would need to be supplemented by some nonprocedural account of how to manage the states of affairs arrived at in the aftermath of the commission of procedurally unjust acts. Elsewhere I have demonstrated (in the context of a theoretical example) that notwithstanding the effective prohibition of discrimination in contract, historically engendered economic differences between racial groups can persist indefinitely when discrimination in contact continues to be practiced (see Loury 1977 and 1995). That is, nondiscrimination, once having been established in the sphere of contract but not in the sphere of contact, can admit of an indefinite perpetuation of the racial inequality originally engendered by historical contractual discrimination. Stated in terms of the language just introduced, this demonstration implies that the colorblindness derived from the Anonymity Axiom—treat all subjects interchangeably and take note of no person's racial identity in the execution of social choice—when viewed as a procedural account of racial justice, is not closed to moral deviation. This, then, is the basis of my larger argument that, as a matter of social ethics, policies should be undertaken to mitigate the economic marginality of an historically stigmatized racial group like black Americans. *This is not an argument for reparations. When the developmental prospects of an individual depend on the circumstances of those with whom he or she is socially affiliated, and when racial stigma continues to operate, even a minimal commitment to equality of opportunity for individuals requires such policies.*

AFFIRMATIVE ACTION AND THE POVERTY OF PROCEDURALISM

The current policy debate over racial preferences in higher education, while not the most significant racial justice question facing the nation today, is nonetheless worth considering here. I incline toward the view that the affirmative action debate receives too much attention in public discourses about racial inequality, obscuring as much as it clarifies. However, by exploring some aspects of this hotly contested public question, I hope to illustrate more incisively the conceptual distinctions that drive my larger argument.[6]

In their study *The Shape of the River,* William Bowen

and Derek Bok, two former Ivy League university presidents, argue that administrators of the great educational philanthropies in the United States should be able to pursue more racial diversity in their undergraduate enrollments as a vitally important educational goal (Bowen and Bok 1998). They offer data to suggest that, through the prudent use of racial identity in the admissions process, this objective is now being achieved by many institutions, and at a tolerable cost. Their evidence persuades me, though, of course, reasonable people can differ on this point. But, in the main, this controversy does not turn on the facts, and it will not be resolved by more or better evidence. Rather, at the core of this argument is a dispute over the very idea that *racial* integration in elite higher education is a good thing.

One might well ask why such an evidently progressive goal should be so controversial. I see two reasons: First, the goals openly espoused by prestigious colleges and universities are inevitably indicative of the larger, collective ideals animating the nation. (And, in light of their considerable influence on national life and culture, this is no less the case for the private than for the public institutions. What a Harvard or Princeton strives after is necessarily, to some degree, what America seeks.) That this society remains a deeply flawed one as long as black Americans are not fully included in its upper reaches is a notion which no longer garners universal assent. Second, the plain fact is that access to elite higher education dramatically enhances one's chances to acquire influence in our putatively meritocratic society.

Competition for a relatively few seats at the table of power is keen, and many chafe at the idea of their child's place being taken by someone "undeserving."

So the process of selecting those who will enter the prestigious colleges and universities is a visible, high-stakes civic exercise. And the perceived legitimacy of these annual "selection rituals" is a matter of vital public interest. As I have noted, two normative concerns are at play in the struggle to define "legitimacy" here—race-blindness and race-egalitarianism. Among the most important conclusions emerging from *The Shape of the River* is that, though not mutually inconsistent, these two ideals are in tension with each other: It is often the case that violating race-blindness can powerfully abet the pursuit of racial equality. This is because, given the differences in test-score distributions among blacks and whites, achieving racial integration at highly selective colleges requires that the chance of being admitted, given a student's test scores, be higher for black than for white applicants. As a matter of simple logic, a college with limited places to fill can achieve more racial diversity only if some black applicants are admitted who would otherwise have been rejected, while some nonblack applicants are rejected who would otherwise have been admitted. Selective institutions will naturally try to reject the least qualified of the otherwise admissible nonblack applicants while admitting the most qualified of those black applicants who would otherwise have been rejected. Yet, in doing so, the college necessarily uses a racially preferential admissions policy. Thus, with resources limited, and with a college committed to remaining highly selective, the two normative concerns come clearly into conflict. A choice between them must be made.

Now, the relevant point for the purposes of this argument turns on the conceptual distinction between procedural and egalitarian moral interests. To develop this point, I suggest a terminological convention: Let us reserve the phrase "race-blind" to describe the practice of not using race when carrying out a policy. And let us employ a different term—"race-indifferent"—to identify the practice of not thinking about race when determining the goals and objectives on behalf of which some policy is adopted. If a selection rule for college admissions can be applied without the racial identity of applicants being known, call that rule "race-blind." In contrast, if a selection rule is chosen with no concern as to what impact it might have upon the various racial groups, then call that rule "race-indifferent." My fundamental claim is that the most important moral questions in matters of race are about indifference, not blindness (which is not to deny, of course, that "blindness questions" can sometimes matter a great deal).

The utility of distinguishing between indifference and blindness becomes clear when one considers that both ameliorating the social disadvantage of blacks and exacerbating this disadvantage can alike be achieved with race-blind policies. Yet whereas a race-blind policy explicitly intended to harm blacks could never be morally acceptable, such policies adopted for the purpose of reducing racial inequality are commonplace, and uncontroversial. Put differently, given the facts of U.S. history, departures from race-indifference are, and should be, evaluated asymmetrically: Those harmful to blacks are widely held to be suspect, whereas non-indifferent undertakings that assist blacks are widely recognized as necessary to the attainment of just social policy.

For example, when a court ruling forbade the practice of affirmative action in college admissions in Texas, the legislature responded by guaranteeing a place at any public university to the top ten percent of every high school class in the state. This so-called ten percent rule mainly benefits students with low test scores and good grades at less competitive high schools—disproportionately blacks and Hispanics—and certainly this was the intent. That is, this rule, while being race-blind, is most decidedly not race-indifferent. Thus we have a situation in Texas in which the explicit use of race in a college admissions formula is forbidden, while the intentional use of a proxy for race publicly adopted so as to reach a similar result is allowed. Can there be any doubt, had a different race-blind proxy been adopted in order to *exclude* black and Hispanic students from public institutions in Texas, that this would be morally unacceptable?

This example illustrates why the key moral issues having to do with race are most often about indifference, not blindness: On the whole, most citizens in the United States see reversing the effects of a history of immoral race relations as a good thing and perpetuating those effects as a bad thing. The choice of instruments to pursue these ends is often of less moment than the choice among the ends themselves.

Indeed, this is so in other policy areas as well: The primary normative concern is not racial discrimination as such, but rather involves deciding how much account to take of racially disparate consequences when choosing among what may be alternative, nondiscriminatory policies. Consider some typical policy dilemmas:

1. Where should a new public facility be located—in the urban center or at the periphery?
2. How will a county's governing commissioners be selected—by elections at the local district level, or from a countywide competition?
3. What protocol should govern the use of deadly force by police officers—shoot whenever feeling threatened, or only when one's life seems to be in the gravest danger?
4. Should a school's history curriculum stress the glories of European exploration and settlement, or the horrors visited upon indigenous peoples by that settlement?

To insist on *indifference* to race when approaching these questions is to evidence both political stupidity and a willful disregard of the concerns of social justice. But to insist on *blindness* to race is also inadequate as a guide to policy. Just as worthy racial goals can sometimes be effectively pursued with race-blind means, so too, a race-transcending public goal is sometimes best pursued with non-race-blind (shall we say "race-sighted"?) means.

Consider, to further illustrate, a state's governor who seeks to appoint judges to the courts. He might reason as follows:

> I need to have a diverse group of appointees both for my own political protection and in the long-term interest of preserving the legitimacy of the administration of justice in this jurisdiction. If I appoint all white men, even though they appear to be the best qualified, not only might I do damage to my reputation, I might also cause some people to doubt that the courts will treat them fairly, thereby undermining public confidence in legal institutions. One of my responsibilities as governor is to ensure that this does not occur.

Maintaining the courts' institutional legitimacy is not a racial goal; it is something everybody has a stake in. And yet, in order to do it, a governor might have to take racial identity into account to see whether his list of possible appointees contains a sufficient number of racial minority group members.

In contrast, consider a federal anti-drug policy concentrating on arresting street-level traffickers and putting them away for a long time. This is a race-blind policy, formulated to pursue nonracial public ends, but one having pronounced racially unequal results. Such policies have led to the incarceration of young people of color in vastly disproportionate numbers—young people, it might be argued, who to some degree are engaged in the illicit traffic precisely because they are at the margin of society and their alternative opportunities are scant.[7] As a result of this and similar policies, out of the 2 million people under lock and key on any given day in the United States, some 1.2 million are blacks, though blacks are only about one-eighth of the national population. A concern solely for the race-blindness of policy instruments—Are the police and the courts applying the laws without racial discrimination?—would fail to raise the larger question: Is this not a public policy that should be examined because of the cost it is imposing on a particular community?

Of course, the example of U.S. anti-drug policy is controversial, but at a minimum reasonable people must accept the central logical claim here: that this race-blind policy instrument raises a question of social justice, the answer to which turns in part on the policy's racially disproportionate effects.[8] And it is *this* distinction—between "blindness" and "indifference"—that I seek to emphasize, because one can slide quickly from a forceful critique of race-sighted policy instruments (arguing that they should be *race-blind*) into a denial of the legitimacy of any discussion of public issues that is formulated in racial terms (arguing that such discussions should be *race-indifferent*).

With these concepts in hand, it is now easier to see the relevance of the affirmative action controversy to my larger claims about the limitations of liberal individualism. The deep questions here are these: When should we explicitly undertake to reduce racial disparities, and what are the means most appropriately employed in pursuit of that end? My argument asserts an ordering of moral concerns, racial justice before race-blindness. I hold that departures from "blindness" undertaken to promote racial equality ought not be barred as a matter of principle. Instead, race-sighted policies should be undertaken, or not, as the result of prudential judgments made on a case-by-case basis. The broad acceptance of this view in U.S. society would have profound consequences. When prestigious institutions use affirmative action to ration access to their ranks, they tacitly and publicly confirm this ordering of moral priorities, in a salient and powerful way. This confirmation is the key civic lesson projected into American national life by these disputed policies. At bottom, what the argument over racial preference, in college admissions and elsewhere, is really about is this struggle for priority among competing public ideals. This is a struggle of crucial importance to the overall discourse on race and social justice in the United States.

Fundamentally, it is because these elite institutions are not "indifferent" to the racial effects of their policies that they have opted not to be "blind" to the racial identities of their applicants. If forced to be race-blind, they can pursue their race-egalitarian goals by other (in all likelihood, less efficient) means. Ought they to do so? Anyone interested in racial justice needs to answer this question. Liberal individualism provides little useful guidance here.

The priority of concerns I am asserting has far-reaching consequences. It implies, for example, that an end to formal discrimination against blacks in this post–civil rights era should in no way foreclose a vigorous public discussion about racial justice. More subtly, elevating racial equality above race-blindness as a normative concern inclines us to think critically, and with greater nuance, about the value of race-blindness. It reminds us that the demand for race-blindness—our moral queasiness about using race in public decisions—has arisen for historically specific reasons, namely slavery and enforced racial segregation over several centuries. These reasons involved the caste-like subordination of blacks—a phenomenon whose effects still linger, and one that was certainly not symmetrical as between the races. As such, taking account of race while trying to mitigate the effects of this subordination, though perhaps ill-advised or unworkable in specific cases, cannot plausibly be seen as the moral equivalent of the discrimination that produced the subjugation of blacks in the first place. To see it that way would be to mire oneself in ahistorical, procedural formalism.

Yet this is precisely what some critics of affirmative action have done, putting forward as their fundamental moral principle the procedural requirement that admissions policies be race-blind. "America, A Race-Free Zone," screams the headline from a recent article by Ward Connerly, who led the successful 1996 ballot campaign against affirmative action in California and is now at the helm of a national organization working to promote similar initiatives in other jurisdictions. Mr. Connerly wants to rid the nation of what he calls "those disgusting little boxes"—the ones applicants check to indicate their racial identities. He and his associates see the affirmative action dispute as an argument between people like themselves, who seek simply to eliminate discrimination, and people like the authors of *The Shape of the River,* who want permission to discriminate if doing so helps the right groups.[9]

This way of casting the question is very misleading. *It obscures from view the most vital matter at stake in the contemporary debate on race and social equity—whether public purposes formulated explicitly in racial terms (that is, violating race-indifference) are morally legitimate, or even morally required.* Anti-preference advocates suggest not, arguing from the premise that an individual's race has no moral relevance to the race-indifferent conclusion that it is either wrong or unnecessary to formulate public purposes in racial terms. But this argument is a *non sequitur.* Moral irrelevance does not imply instrumental irrelevance. Nor does the conviction that an individual's race is irrelevant to an assessment of that individual's worth require the conclusion that patterns of unequal racial representation in important public venues are irrelevant to an assessment of the moral health of our society.

The failure to make these distinctions is dangerous, for it leads inexorably to doubts about the validity of discussing social justice issues in the United States in racial terms at all. Or, more precisely, it reduces such a discussion to the narrow ground of assessing whether or not certain policies are race-blind. Whatever the anti-preference crusaders may intend, and however desirable in the abstract may be their colorblind ideal, their campaign is having the effect of devaluing our collective and still unfinished efforts to achieve greater equality between the races. Americans are now engaged in deciding whether the pursuit of racial equality will continue in the century ahead to be a legitimate and vitally important purpose in our public life. Increasingly, doubts are being expressed about this. *Fervency for race-blindness has left some observers simply blind to a basic fact of American public life: We have pressing moral dilemmas in our society that can be fully grasped only when viewed against the backdrop of our unlovely racial history.*

"FIGMENT OF THE PIGMENT" OR "ENIGMA OF THE STIGMA"?

Consider the stubborn social reality of race-consciousness in U.S. society. A standard concern about racial preferences in college admissions is that they promote an unhealthy fixation on racial identity among students. By classifying by race, it is said, we distance ourselves further from the goal of achieving a race-blind society. Many proponents of race-blindness as the primary moral ideal come close to equating the use of racial information in administrative practices with the continued awareness of racial identity in the broad society. They come close, that is, to collapsing the distinction between racial *information* and racial *identity*. Yet consciousness of race in the society at large is a matter of subjective states of mind, involving how people understand themselves and how they perceive others. It concerns the extent to which race is taken into account in the intimate social lives of citizens. The implicit assumption of advocates of race-blindness is that, if we would just stop putting people into these boxes, they would oblige us by not thinking of themselves in these terms. But this assumption is patently false. Anti-preference advocates like to declare that we cannot get beyond race while taking race into account—as if someone has proven a theorem to this effect. But no such demonstration is possible.

The conservative scholars Stephan and Abigail Thernstrom, in their influential study *America in Black and White*, provide an example of this tendency of thought. They blame race-conscious public policies for what they take to be an excess of racial awareness among blacks. Affirmative action, they argue, induces blacks to seek political benefits from racial solidarity. This, in turn, encourages a belief by blacks in what they call "the figment of the pigment"—the conviction that, for African Americans, race is a trait that is inexorably and irrevocably different from European or Asian ethnicity (Thernstrom and Thernstrom 1997, p. 535). This gets it exactly backwards, in my view. It is not the use of race as a criterion of public action that causes blacks to nurture a sense of racial otherness. Rather, it is the historical fact and the specific nature of blacks' racial otherness that causes affirmative action—when undertaken to benefit blacks—to be so fiercely contested in contemporary American politics.

To see what I am getting at here, consider the following thought experiment: Few people, upon entering a shop with the sign "Smith and Sons" in the window to encounter a youngish proprietor at the counter, will begin to worry that they are about to be served by an unqualified beneficiary of nepotism. But I venture that a great many people, upon seeing a black as part of their treatment team at a top-flight hospital, may be led to consider the possibility that, because of affirmative action in medical school admissions, they are about to be treated by an unqualified doctor. Yet supposing that some preference had, in fact, been given in both cases and bearing in mind the incentives created by the threat of a malpractice suit, the objective probability that a customer will receive lower-quality service in the former situation is likely to be greater than the chance that a patient will receive lower-quality treatment in the latter. This difference between reality and perception has little to do with political principles, and everything to do with racial stigma.

Moreover, the ongoing experience of racial stigma is what causes many blacks to see racial solidarity as an existential necessity. Perhaps I could put it this way: It's not *the figment of the pigment*, it is *the enigma of the stigma* that causes race to be so salient for blacks today. Now mind you, I have already stipulated (in Axioms 1 and 2) that, at the most fundamental level, the "pigment" is a "figment." I have rejected racial essentialism. But I also have argued that, notwithstanding the arbitrariness of racial markers, the classifying of persons on the basis of such markers is an inescapable social-cognitive activity. And I have suggested that such markers could be invested with powerful social meanings—that meaning-hungry agents could build elaborate structures of self-definition around them.

So after centuries of intensive racial classification we are now confronted with raced subjects demanding to be recognized as such. Here are selves endogenous to the historical and cultural flow, who see their social world partly through the lens of their "pigment," and the best some critics can do by way of a response is to dismiss them as deluded, confused believers in a "figment." ("Why are they so obsessed with race? Can't they see it was all a big mistake?") Would-be moralists, even some blacks (Kennedy 1997), are puzzled and disturbed at the specter of African Americans being proud of the accomplishments, and ashamed of the failures, of their co-racialists.[10] And those to whom the "wages of whiteness" flow like manna from heaven, who have a race but never have to think about it, can blithely declare, "It's time to move on."

This is simplistic social ethics and sophomoric social psychology, it seems to me. And it is an especially odd position for a liberal individualist to take. I have always supposed that the core idea of liberalism is to credit the dignity of human beings. Yet when those subjected to racial stigma, having managed to construct a more or less dignified self-concept out of the brute facts of an imposed categorization, confront us with their "true" selves—perhaps as believers in the need to carry forward a tradition of racial struggle inherited from their forebears, or as proponents of a program of racial self-help—they are written off as benighted adherents of a discredited creed. We would never tell the antagonists in a society divided by religion that the way to move forward is for the group in the minority to desist from worshiping their false god. But this, in effect, is what many critics today are saying to black Americans who simply refuse to "get over it."

The basic point needing emphasis here is this: The use of race-based instruments is typically the result, rather than the cause, of the wider awareness of racial identity in society. This is why race-blindness is such a superficial moral ideal: To forgo cognizance of race, out of fear that others will be encouraged to think in racial terms, is a bit like closing the barn door after the horses have gone. One cannot grasp the workings of the social order in which we are embedded in the United States without making use of racial categories, because these socially constructed categories are etched in the consciousness of the individuals with whom we must reckon. Because they use race to articulate their self-understandings, we must be mindful of race as we conduct our public affairs. This is a *cognitive,* not a *normative* point. One can agree with the liberal individualist claim that race is irrelevant to an individual's moral worth, that individuals and not groups are the bearers of rights, and nevertheless affirm that, to deal effectively with these autonomous individuals, account must be taken of the categories of thought in which they understand themselves.

Indeed, it is easy to produce compelling examples in which the failure to take race into account serves to exacerbate racial awareness. Consider the extent to which our public institutions are regarded as legitimate by all the people. When a public executive (like the hypothetical governor considered earlier) recognizes the link between the perceived legitimacy of institutions and their degree of racial representation, and acts on that recognition, he or she is acting so as to *inhibit*, not to *heighten*, the salience of race in public life. When the leaders of elite educational philanthropies attempt to bring a larger number of black youngsters into their ranks, so as to increase the numbers of their graduates from these communities, they are acting in a similar fashion. *To acknowledge that institutional legitimacy can turn on matters of racial representation is to recognize a basic historical fact about the American national community, not to make a moral error.* The U.S. Army has long understood this.[11] It is absurd to hold that this situation derives from the existence of selection rules—in colleges and universities, in the military, or anywhere else—that take account of race.

So much may seem too obvious to warrant stating but, sadly, it is not. In the 5th U.S. Circuit Court of Appeals *Hopwood* opinion, Judge Smith questions the diversity rationale for using racial preferences in higher education admissions.[12] He argues that, because a college or university exists to promote the exchange of ideas, defining diversity in racial terms necessarily entails the pernicious belief that blacks think one way, whites another. But this argument is fallacious for reasons just stated. Suppose one begins with the contrary premise, that there is no "black" or "white" way of thinking. Suppose further that conveying this view to one's students is a high pedagogic goal. The students being keenly aware of their respective racial identities, some racial diversity may be required to achieve the pedagogic goal. Teaching that "not all blacks think alike" will be much easier when there are enough blacks around to show their diversity of thought. More generally, *conveying effectively the ultimate moral irrelevance of race in our society may require functional attention by administrative personnel to the racial composition of the learning environment. Whether, and to what extent, this may be so is a prudential, not a principled, question. It cannot be resolved a priori.*

AN APPROPRIATE VENUE FOR COLORBLINDNESS

There is, however, an objection to be raised to the position being developed here. At the consequentialist level, a critic may concede that some departures from colorblindness are needed, though they should be "narrowly tailored" to meet only the most "compelling interest" as the language of recent Supreme Court rulings on affirmative action would have it. But at the most profound moral level, doesn't someone who abhors the consequences of racial stigma have to affirm a kind of moral blindness to the race of agents? I think this is in fact the case, and I am not the least bit reluctant to say so, but I continue to urge clarity on this point.

Let us distinguish among three domains or venues of public action in a racially stratified society where the "blindness" intuitions of liberal neutrality might be applied.

First is the domain of *policy implementation*—where we decide on the instruments of public action. Here we are admitting students to college or hiring public employees or distributing social benefits. Some mechanism is being used to do this, and that mechanism may, or may not, take cognizance of a subject's race. "Blindness" here means structuring public conduct so that people from different racial groups who are otherwise similar can expect similar treatment. This is what most people have in mind when they insist that the government should be "colorblind."

Second is the domain of *policy evaluation*—where we assess the consequences of public action. Here we are deciding whether to build a prison or a school, and if it is a school, whether it should serve the general population or only the most accomplished students. We are fighting a war on drugs and deciding whether to concentrate on the buying or the selling side of illicit transactions. As a general matter, prior to choosing a course of public action we need to assess the relative costs and benefits of the alternatives before us. The impact of an alternative on particular racial groups may, or may not, be explicitly reckoned in this assessment. "Blindness" here means not seeing a policy as more or less desirable on account of the race of those affected. This is what the Anonymity Axiom of social choice theory requires.

Third is what I will call the domain of *civic construction*—where we develop our nation's sense of shared purpose and common fate. Here we are building monuments, constructing public narratives, enacting rituals, and, most generally, pursuing policies that have an inescapably expressive as well as a directly instrumental effect. "Blindness" to race in this domain means deploying the instruments of civic pedagogy so as to promote a sense of national community that transcends racial divisions. This is what my Axiom 2 (on anti-essentialism) requires, when it is embraced without reference to empirical assessments.

Veterans of the racial preferences wars are most familiar with the questions—having mainly to do with the unfairness of racial discrimination—that arise in the domain of implementation. To get a glimpse of the subtle dilemmas that arise in the domain of evaluation, imagine that the central bank is trying to decide whether or not to induce a recession, so as to lower the risk of inflation. Would it be legitimate to tolerate a somewhat greater chance of inflation while maintaining a strong demand for labor because doing so also manages to hold the unemployment rate of black youth at humane levels for the first time in a half-century? Can we reckon that this is a good policy because it contributes to overcoming racial stigma, draws blacks more fully into the mainstream of society, and permits them to earn the respect of their fellow citizens? (Here I mean to suggest that, but for this racial benefit, a different decision might be taken.) In other words, can we explicitly count as a benefit to society what we calculate to be the racially progressive consequences (reducing black economic marginality) of what is a race-blind action (electing to take a greater risk of inflation)?

The issues arising in the domain of civic construction are also subtle. Consider the practice of capital punishment, which may or may not deter murder, but which is most definitely the state-sanctioned killing of a human being. Would it be legitimate when deciding whether or not to undertake the powerfully symbolic public ritual of executing lawbreakers to take note of what may be a large racial disparity in its application? (Here I am supposing for the sake of argument that the processes of policing, judging, and sentencing that lead to persons being executed are not racially biased, and I am asking whether we might nevertheless question the use of capital punishment because of its racially disproportionate effects.) In other words, must we be "blind" to the possibility that such a racial imbalance could distort our civic self-understanding in the United States?

Or, to take a very different case, consider the conscious act of integrating by race the elite who exercise power and who bear honor in the society—the people to whom we delegate discretion over our lives. Suppose we undertake to ensure that there are, visibly, African Americans among that elite. Suppose this goal is pursued not to bestow benefits on black people, as such, but with the specific intent of integrating the national community by rubbing out in the consciousness of the populace a perception of racial difference in inherent capacities or deserved social standing. Would that be a valid enterprise? Such a project, after all, pays tribute to the idea of race-blindness, too: It seeks to diminish the sense within the polity that we consist of racial groups that are differently endowed or unequally worthy of respect, with some more deserving than others of inclusion in the prized venues of public life.

We have, then, these three domains—implementation, evaluation, and civic construction—giving rise to three classes of public questions: How should we treat individuals? How should we choose the goals to be pursued through our policies? And how much awareness ought we to have of the ways in which the conduct of public business can perpetuate into yet another generation the inherited stigma of race?

Liberal individualism seems to militate strongly in favor of "blindness" in both the first and the second domains. I believe this is wrong on both counts, because it is ahistorical and sociologically naïve. Race-blind proceduralism fails, I have suggested, because (among other reasons) it is not closed to moral deviation. And a principled stand of race-indifference is unacceptable as well, I have argued, because it rules out policies that are almost universally credited as being necessary and proper to combat the lingering effects of past racial discrimination. Given U.S. history, few thoughtful people are prepared to import their love of the race-blind principle into the domain of evaluation. They may object to race-based selection rules, but they do not object to the pursuit of explicitly race-egalitarian outcomes through public policies that take no notice of race at the point of implementation (like the ten percent plan in Texas). That is, though they may embrace race-*blindness* they reject race-*indifference.* Thus, for example, there is much (I think plausible) disquiet at the thought of constructing race-based electorates for the purpose of giving blacks greater political voice, but hardly any opposition to moving from at-large to non-racially drawn single-member voting districts when the intent is to produce a similar outcome.

I want to suggest that only in the domain of civic construction should some notion of race-blindness be elevated to the level of fundamental principle. The operative moral idea would be what the sociologist Orlando Patterson has called the principle of infrangibility (that is, the absence of boundary)—saying that we are One Nation, Indivisible, and taking that idea seriously enough to try to act (whether in a race-blind or a race-sighted fashion) so as to bring that circumstance about. Those people languishing at the margins, even if they are strange and threatening, are to be seen, in the ways that most fundamentally count for our politics and civic life, as being essentially like us. We're going to prudentially and constitutionally, but determinedly and expeditiously, move so as to tear down, or certainly build no higher, the boundaries of race that divide the body politic.

Thus when elite college presidents who practice race-preferential admissions say, in effect, "While administering multi-billion-dollar philanthropies that enjoy (for the public good) the protection of tax exemption, we endeavor, among other things, to construct an elite leadership cadre of African Americans at the end of the twentieth and the beginning of the twenty-first century," they say a very modest thing. In the elite schools studied by Bowen and Bok (1998), the average admissions rate for whites is about 25 percent. Getting rid of all the affirmative action is calculated to raise that rate to about 27 percent. So for every 75 whites rejected under the regime of race-preferential admissions currently being practiced, 73 would still be rejected after the eradication of affirmative action. Why, then, all the energy, why all the angst, why all the hand wringing, why all the clamor, why all the concern that America is being run aground, that our standards are being trashed, that the barbarians are at the gates? Why such resistance when, as the data in Bowen and Bok's book strongly suggest, the boundary of racial hierarchy is being erased just a little bit by the trickling few black students who, at the margin and because of the colleges' practice of affirmative action, are being inducted into the leadership cadres of the United States?

Conversely, why is there so little alarm at the enormous racial disparity in the rates of imprisonment experienced by young American men? Why is it that, when a black American scholar of unquestioned competence and respectable intellectual pedigree raises this question, he can be accused of "playing the race card"—that is, of letting his sense of racial loyalty take precedence over his commitment to promote universal public goals? In a society that loves justice and that has a troubled racial history, like the United States, is not avoiding the further demonization of disadvantaged and socially isolated inner-city black youth a public purpose of trans-racial significance?

I hold that there is nothing in political liberalism, rightly understood, that should lead us to reject that public goal. There is nothing wrong with a liberal, concerned about social justice, undertaking to fight racial stigma. There is nothing wrong with constructing a racially integrated elite in America. There is nothing wrong with fretting over 1.2 million African-American young bodies under the physical control of the state. Indeed, I am led to wonder how any thoughtful person aware of the history and the contemporary structure of U.S. society could conclude otherwise.

5

CONCLUSIONS

LET US review the bidding: By now the reader knows that I take a constructivist position in regard to the ontological status of "race": A field of human subjects characterized by morphological variability comes through concrete historical experience to be partitioned into subgroups defined by some cluster of physical markers. Information-hungry agents hang expectations around these markers, beliefs that can, by processes I have discussed in some detail, become self-confirming. Meaning-hungry agents invest these markers with social, psychological, and even spiritual significance. Race-markers come to form the core of personal and social identities. Narrative accounts of descent are constructed around them. And so groups of subjects, identifying with one another, sharing feelings of pride, (dis)honor, shame, loyalty, and hope—and defined in some measure by their holding these race-markers in common—come into existence. This vesting of reasonable expectation and ineffable meaning in objectively arbitrary markings on human bodies comes to be reproduced over the generations, takes on a social life of its own, seems natural and not merely conventional, and ends up having profound consequences for social relations among individuals in the raced society.

The reader also knows that I am committed to the position of anti-essentialism. My emphasis on the conventional and not natural character of race is accompanied by a conviction that no deep-seated, inherent inequality of human potential as between the members of different racial groups exists. And so I can credit no appeal to essential difference as an ultimate explanation of African-American social disadvantage. This belief in anti-essentialism calls me to a ministry of racial apologetics—defending my faith in Axiom 2. But it also makes me keenly aware of the presence among my fellow citizens of infidels and apostates—people who, in a not necessarily conscious manner, give credence to the essentialist view. Confronted by the facts of racially disparate achievement, the racially disproportionate transgression of legal strictures, and racially unequal development of productive potential, observers need to give an account. They need to tell themselves a "story," to adopt some "model" of what has generated their data, to embrace some framework for gauging how best to respond. In effect, observers must answer the question, Where does the problem lie, with US or with THEM? Their willingness to examine whether taken-for-granted civic arrangements in fact correspond to their nation's professed ideals depends upon the answers they give to this question. Indeed, the very processes of social cognition and discernment, the awareness of anomaly and capacity for empathy, the stirrings of conscience in a society will, I have argued, be influenced by widely held beliefs in this regard.

Faced with manifestations of extreme marginality and dysfunction among some of the racially marked, will the citizenry indignantly cry out, "What manner of people are THEY, who languish in that way?" Or will they be moved, perhaps after overcoming an instinctual revulsion, to ask, reflectively and reflexively, "What manner of people are WE who accept such degradation in our midst?" I have argued that the attainment of racial justice depends crucially on which narrative is settled upon. Reform becomes possible only when this second question is posed.

Readers who have persisted to this point know that I hold the latter response to be less probable, and that I expect this response to come less easily to an external observer's mind when the raced group in question is stigmatized in that observer's perception. *Racial stigma, then, promotes the tacit presumption of an essentialist cause for racial inequality, ascribing to blacks (in the case at hand) the virtual social identity that they are, in some sense, "damaged goods."* While I am undisturbed at the use of the term "racism" in reference to stigmatization of this sort, I am also unenlightened by it.

Given my anti-essentialist commitment, I am keen to distinguish between two accounts of the problem of persisting racial inequality. One account gives pride of place to racial discrimination. The other makes racial stigma the main concern. I have argued in favor of the latter account—relatively speaking, not taking that position in an absolutist way—for two reasons. As an empirical judgment, I hold that reward bias (unequal returns to equally productive contributors) based on race is now less important in accounting for the disparate social outcomes that history has bequeathed to us than is development bias (unequal chances to realize one's productive potential) based on race. As a moral judgment, I hold that there is a fundamental tension between the ideal of attaining racial justice and that of respecting individual autonomy: Given our history in the United States, autonomous individuals will elect to practice discrimination in contact. Yet the inevitable consequence of such racially preferential social intercourse, I have argued, is to impair the developmental opportunities of a racially stigmatized group like African Americans.

The idea of discrimination points mainly to reward bias, telling us little that is useful about the practice of racial preference in associative behavior. The stigma idea is more flexible, providing insight both into race-constrained social interactions and race-influenced processes of social cognition. Thinking in terms of stigma helps us to better understand the operations of causal feedback loops that can perpetuate racial inequality from one generation to the next.

SOME THOUGHTS ON THE POSSIBILITY OF RACIAL REFORM

The idealized social interactions that I have employed in this book to analyze the problem of racial inequality involve an observer and a subject being observed. (This can, in one important and interesting case, be understood reflexively, such that the observer and the subject coincide.) Race is a cluster of marks on the bodies of subjects to which subjects and observers attach expectations and meanings. The "stereotype models" of Chapter 2 were designed to show, in the context of these subject-observer interactions, how expectations (information) come to be embedded in the race-markers via self-confirming feedback loops. With the "stigma models" of Chapter 3 I explored how meanings are attached to the race-markers (meanings about identity, identification, ideals, worthiness).

The difference between racial stigma and racial stereotyping might be thought of in the following way: Whereas stereotyping concerns an observer's anticipation of acts that are thought to be associated with, but are not necessarily coextensive with, the subject, stigma invokes the observer's (perhaps not consciously acknowledged) perception of qualities thought to be essential to the make-up of the subject. (In principle, the attached meanings need not be derogatory, though in the context at hand—race in the United States—they most often will be.) Basically, what I want to invoke with the notion of "stigma" is some kind of "meta-belief," a matter more of "specification" than of "inference," a belief by the observer (or the subject!) about the subject's intrinsic nature which conditions how other more specific pieces of evidence involving the subject will be interpreted.

Let us suppose that social outcomes (inequality, mobility, performance) for subjects depend on the qualities of "structures," the nature of subjects, and the behaviors of subjects and observers. "Structures" are of two kinds:

1. External—civic, public—providing opportunity and rewards, and influenced by policies that are determined in the larger society, through politics (public schools, rules governing market transactions, policies of social provision, and so on).

2. Non-external—communal, private—influenced by an in-group "culture" that mediates relations between subjects and the opportunity provided through external structures, and "governed" via expressive and associative actions within communities of subjects, who can now function as self-observers as well (religious institutions, advocacy organizations, peer groups, and so on).

Now, faced with the durable inequality of race-marked subjects, observers need to figure out what has gone wrong. The possibilities are threefold:

1. External structures have failed (to afford fair opportunity for development or reward for achievement).

2. Non-external structures have failed (to provide appropriate opportunity for development).

3. The essential nature of the race-marked subjects precludes development.

Meaningful equality of citizenship requires that (3) be ruled out by axiom (non-essentialism) and that (1) be remedied via reform wherever possible. (This is not a bad short definition of "racial justice.") Out-group observers who credit (3) are disinclined to examine the possibility of (1). In-group subject-observers who credit (1) are disinclined to examine the possibility of (2), especially if they fear that some outsiders credit (3), or, in the tragic but not to be dismissed case, if they themselves credit the possibility of (3).

The apostates and infidels who are unmoved by the "sermon" I have offered here on behalf of racial apologetics credit (3). The social-cognitively challenged agents in the thought experiments of Chapters 2 and 3 (the policeman who thinks "If they look alike, they act alike"; the monopolistic employer who thinks "Those people just don't make good workers") are impeded from perceiving the possibility of (1) by their (perhaps partial) crediting of (3). Black civil society heroes (inner-city Christian pastors, black Muslims working in prisons) may practice "pro-black discrimination in contact" in the service of looking into and remedying (2).

One can ask whether it is necessary for race-marked insiders who want to ensure that (1) is remedied to deny that (3) is widely believed, even when it is. That is Charles Mills's charge against the Frederick Douglass of 1852. Most of the

Founders, who incorporated slavery into the republic, Mills says, believed (3) and did nothing to remedy (1). Yet Douglass broke with the abolitionist William Lloyd Garrison when the latter insisted that the Constitution was a "compact with death." Douglass idealized the Founding, denying that it could be tainted by belief in (3). Was this necessary?

Notice that outside observers of the race-marked group can intervene only to address (1), and this will be ineffective if mainly (2) or (3) is true. Observing that they reject (1) is not to establish that they accept (3). Thus one need not impute belief in (3) to the editorial writer for *American Enterprise* magazine mentioned in Chapter 3 for the force of my criticism to stand. One need only impute to him an unwillingness to explore (1) as fully as it deserves to be explored, an unwillingness he may feel because he believes (2). So a way to translate my criticism into the language of this concluding chapter would be to insist that these outside observers have a civic duty to explore (1) until all avenues are exhausted, even if they do believe (2), and indeed, perhaps especially if they do.

Notice further that insider race-marked subject-observers can mainly address (2), though of course they can remonstrate and agitate on behalf of (1). But if these (now pathetic) insiders themselves credit (3), they may, in the madness of their self-contempt, be induced to deny this to their conscious selves, and become rabid advocates of (1), accusing every outsider in sight of believing (3). Outsiders who do not believe (3), but who are unwilling to bear the duties of citizenship associated with exploring and remedying (1), will talk about (2) all the time. This will make life difficult for insiders who reject (3) as well, but who know that, while (2) may be a part of the question, unless (1) is fixed the oppressive weight of history on their group will not be removed. If they now openly advocate for (2), they lend aid and comfort to the duty-shirking outsiders.

Civic-minded outsiders, who do not credit (3) at all but who think too little attention is being paid to (2), may be reluctant to listen to insider arguments for exploration and remedy of (1). And communally responsible insiders, who know that (2) needs attention but who think the larger polity has abandoned its responsibility to look into (1), may withdraw in despair or rage. Finally, the role of the responsible race-marked public intellectual of today (say, a race-marked subject-observer like me) might be understood as follows. Keep both (1) and (2) in play, finding a way to make reform in either sphere complement that in the other.

I'm frankly more concerned that (3) is a widespread view. It is unhelpful to call someone who believes in (3) a "racist," though that description is not necessarily wrong. In the quotation in Chapter 3 from the *American Enterprise* magazine, and in the article from which it is drawn, the editorialist, Karl Zinsmeister (who, of course, merely stands in here for a host of conservative voices), never allows that either (1) or (2) might account for the problem. And, though he doesn't expressly endorse (3), he expressly defends Charles Murray, who does. This familiar conservative argument amounts to "That I don't credit (1) as worthy of investigation doesn't mean that I don't 'care' about these folks." The reason I resist calling belief in (3) "racism" is that not "caring" is what many people think racism is. So a person will feel insulted by the nonspecific charge of "racism," while continuing to credit (3) or being too lazy to explore fully the possibility of (1).

RACE-EGALITARIANISM BEFORE RACE-BLINDNESS

I have argued that race-blindness—as a purely procedural theory of racial justice—is necessarily insufficient because it cannot cope with the consequences of its own violation. Moreover, in practice the moral criterion of race-blindness fails for a related though distinct reason: Its proponents tend to apply their cherished principle only to a restricted domain of public life—that of policy implementation in formal economic and bureaucratic undertakings. Yet the issue of racial justice, properly conceived, ought not be so limited, and the intuitive appeal of "blindness" as a guiding moral principle is far weaker when applied in the domain of policy evaluation. I drive this point home by contrasting the race-blindness idea with what I have called race-indifference—a disregard for the effects of a policy choice on the welfare of persons in different racial groups. By pointing to a history of racial subordination and the evident importance of race in present-day structures of opportunity in the United States, I make the case that the "indifference" question should be regarded as ethically more fundamental than the "blindness" question, and that race-indifference should be rejected in the American context. This supports my conclusion that, insofar as the concern is the lagging status of African Americans, the quest for social justice should entail a commitment to race-egalitarianism, and that this commitment can properly be pursued through policies (such as but not limited to affirmative action) that may fail to meet the standards of race-blindness, race-indifference, or both.

Finally, I see two big ideas emerging from this argument. The first is the claim that both the analytic and the philosophic resources of liberal individualism are insufficient to generate an understanding of, or to provide an adequate response to, the problem of pronounced and durable social disadvantage among African Americans. I claim that abstract individualism is just not up to the task here—neither the descriptive nor the prescriptive task. The second idea is closely connected with the first. It is, to repeat, the distinction I want to insist be drawn between *racial discrimination* and *racial stigma* in discussions of the problem of social exclusion and economic disadvantage among black Americans.

Discrimination is about how people are treated; stigma is about who, at the deepest cognitive level, they are understood to be. As such, these distinct ways of framing the problem of racial inequality lead to radically distinct intellectual and political programs. A diagnosis of *discrimination* yields a search for harmful or malicious actions as the treatment, using the law and moral suasion to curtail or modify those actions. But seeing *stigma* as the disease inclines one to look for insidious habits of thought, selective patterns of social intercourse, biased processes of social cognition, and defective public deliberations when seeking a cure. Here the limits of conventional legal action and moral suasion, and the need for deeper and more far-reaching structural reform, come clearly into view. To be sure, such reform should redress resource disparities between groups. But it should also attend to the ways in which race-mediated social meanings are constructed, in order to avoid the perpetuation into yet another American generation of the ugly legacy of racial stigma.

These big ideas incline me to the following major conclusion: The unfair treatment of persons based on race in formal economic transactions is no longer the most significant barrier to the full participation of blacks in American life. More important is the fact that too many African Americans cannot gain access on anything approaching equal terms to social resources that are essential for human flourishing, but that are made available to individuals primarily through informal, culturally mediated, race-influenced social intercourse. It follows that achieving racial justice at this point in American history requires more than reforming procedures so as to ensure fair treatment for blacks in the economic and bureaucratic undertakings of private and state actors.

This kind of reform, while necessary, is far from sufficient. Yet it is the only reform that the liberal-individualist morality of race-blindness affords us. I hope to have persuaded the reader with the foregoing argument that a broader and more comprehensive moral vision is required of us—the vision I have called race-egalitarianism. On this view, achieving the elusive goal of racial justice requires that we undertake, as a conscious end of policy, to eliminate the objective disparity in economic and social capacity between the race-segregated networks of affiliation that continue to characterize the social structure of American public life, and that constitute the most morally disturbing remnant of this nation's tortured racial past.

Appendix

Notes

References

Index

APPENDIX

Table 1. Median earnings, 1999, year-round full-time workers, age 25 and older, by education.

	Education				
	Less than high school	High school	Some college	Bachelor's or more	Total
Earnings ($000)					
Men					
Black	22.1	27.4	32.0	42.3	30.9
White	19.4	33.1	38.5	57.3	40.1
Women					
Black	NA	20.6	25.2	36.6	25.1
White	13.8	22.2	26.9	40.4	27.6
Black/white ratio					
Men	1.1	0.8	0.8	0.7	0.8
Women	NA	0.9	0.9	0.9	0.9
Increase over next-lower educational level (%)					
Men					
Black	—	24.0	16.8	32.2	
White	—	70.6	16.3	48.8	
Women					
Black	—	NA	22.3	45.2	
White	—	60.9	21.2	50.2	

Source: U.S. Census Bureau, *Money Income in the United States: 1999*, Current Population Reports, Series P60-209 (Washington, 2000), table 10.

Table 2. Occupations of employed men and women age 16 and older, 1999.

	Men		Women	
Occupation	Black	White	Black	White
Managerial and professional specialty	18.0%	29.5%	24.5%	33.4%
Technical, sales, and administrative support	18.4	19.7	38.2	40.6
Service occupations	17.4	8.9	25.6	16.2
Precision production, craft, and repair	14.3	19.4	2.1	2.1
Operators, fabricators, and laborers	29.8	18.3	9.4	6.5
Farming, forestry, fishing	2.2	4.1	0.2	1.2
Total	100.0	100.0	100.0	100.0

Source: Bureau of Labor Statistics, *Labor Force Statistics from the Current Population Survey,* table 10. <ftp://ftp.bls.gov/pub/special.requests/lf/aat10.txt>

Table 3. Percentage of population below the poverty level, March 1999.

Age	Black			White		
	Worked full time	Worked part time	Did not work	Worked full time	Worked part time	Did not work
16–17	NA	20.2	30.4	4.5	7.2	17.5
18–24	10.2	28.9	43.1	4.9	15.1	31.6
25–34	5.4	29.9	47.4	2.8	14.8	32.0
35–54	3.1	26.0	48.2	1.8	10.5	23.2
55–64	4.7	13.8	34.6	1.5	6.8	18.0
65+	2.0	10.9	25.3	1.9	2.6	9.6

Source: Joseph Dalaker and Bernadette D. Proctor, *Poverty in the United States, 1999*, U.S. Census Bureau, Current Population Reports, Series P60-210 (Washington, 2000), table 3.

Table 4. Asset ownership by income quintile.

	Median net worth (1993 $)			
	1991		1993	
Quintile	Black	White	Black	White
1st	0	10,743	250	7,605
2nd	3,446	26,665	3,406	27,057
3rd	8,302	35,510	8,480	36,341
4th	21,852	55,950	20,745	54,040
5th	56,922	128,298	45,023	123,350
All households	4,844	47,075	4,418	45,740
	Number of households (000s)			
	1991		1993	
Quintile	Black	White	Black	White
1st	4,041	14,480	4,066	14,662
2nd	2,436	16,006	2,663	16,162
3rd	2,124	16,388	2,126	16,591
4th	1,353	17,043	1,454	17,218
5th	814	17,492	937	17,558
All households	10,768	81,409	11,248	82,190

Source: U.S. Census Bureau, *Asset Ownership of Households, 1993,* table F. <www.census.gov/hhes/www/wealth/1993/wlth93f.html>

Table 5. Racial composition of couples, aged 25–34, 1990 (native-born population).

	Race of wife					
Race of husband	White	Black	Hispanic	Asian	American Indian	Total
White	96.2%	0.2%	2.2%	0.9%	0.5%	100%
Black	5.3	91.9	1.7	0.8	0.2	100
Hispanic	33.2	1.1	64.0	1.2	0.4	100
Asian	39.9	0.5	10.2	48.2	1.2	100
American Indian	54.7	1.3	4.0	1.1	38.9	100
	Race of husband					
Race of wife	White	Black	Hispanic	Asian	American Indian	Total
White	97.2%	0.4%	1.7%	0.2%	0.4%	100%
Black	2.1	97.0	0.7	< 0.1	0.1	100
Hispanic	38.7	2.4	57.0	1.0	0.5	100
Asian	70.1	5.0	4.4	19.8	0.7	100
American Indian	57.3	1.7	2.4	0.8	37.8	100

Source: Reynolds Farley, *The New American Reality,* table 6.5. Copyright 1996 Russell Sage Foundation. Used with permission of the Russell Sage Foundation.

Table 6. Average mathematics test scores, National Assessment of Educational Progress Tests.

	Black			White		
Year	Age 9	Age 13	Age 17	Age 9	Age 13	Age 17
1973	190.0	228.0	270.0	225.0	274.0	310.0
1978	192.4	229.6	268.4	224.1	271.6	305.9
1982	194.9	240.4	271.8	224.0	274.4	303.7
1986	201.6	249.2	278.6	226.9	273.6	307.5
1990	208.4	249.1	288.5	235.2	276.3	309.5
1992	208.0	250.2	285.8	235.1	278.9	311.9
1994	212.1	251.5	285.5	236.8	280.8	312.3
1996	211.6	252.1	286.4	236.8	281.2	313.4
1999	210.9	251.0	283.3	238.8	283.1	314.8

Scale from 0 to 500:
150: Simple arithmetic facts
200: Beginning skills and understanding
250: Numerical operations and beginning problem solving
300: Moderately complex procedures and reasoning
350: Multi-step problem solving and algebra

Source: Jay R. Campbell, Catherine M. Hombo, and John Mazzeo, *Three Decades of Student Performance* (Washington: U.S. Department of Education, Office of Educational Research and Improvement, National Center for Education Statistics, 2000), table B.8 and p. 17.

Table 7. Average reading test scores, National Assessment of Educational Progress Tests.

	Black			White		
Year	Age 9	Age 13	Age 17	Age 9	Age 13	Age 17
1971	170.1	222.4	238.7	214	260.9	291.4
1975	181.2	225.7	240.6	216.6	262.1	293
1980	189.3	232.8	243.1	221.3	264.4	292.8
1984	185.7	236.3	264.3	218.2	262.6	295.2
1988	188.5	242.9	274.4	217.7	261.3	294.7
1990	181.8	241.5	267.3	217	262.3	296.6
1992	184.5	237.6	260.6	217.9	266.4	297.4
1994	185.4	234.3	266.2	218	265.1	295.7
1996	190.9	234	266.1	219.6	265.9	295.1
1999	185.5	238.2	263.9	221	266.7	294.6

Scale from 0 to 500:
150: Simple, discrete reading tasks
200: Partially developed skills and understanding
250: Interrelate ideas and make generalizations
300: Understand complicated information
350: Learn from specialized reading materials

Source: Jay R. Campbell, Catherine M. Hombo, and John Mazzeo, *Three Decades of Student Performance* (Washington: U.S. Department of Education, Office of Educational Research and Improvement, National Center for Education Statistics, 2000), table B.9 and p. 18.

Table 8. Life expectancy.

	Men		Women	
	Black	White	Black	White
At birth				
1969–71	60.0	67.9	68.3	75.5
1979–81	64.1	70.8	73.9	78.2
1991	64.6	72.9	73.8	79.6
1998	67.6	74.5	74.8	80.0
At age 1				
1969–71	61.2	68.3	69.4	75.7
1979–81	64.6	70.7	73.3	78.0
1991	64.9	72.5	73.9	79.1
1998	67.7	74.0	74.8	79.4
At age 20				
1969–71	43.5	50.2	51.2	57.2
1979–81	46.5	52.5	54.9	59.4
1991	46.9	54.1	55.4	60.4
1998	49.5	55.5	56.2	60.8
At age 65				
1969–71	12.5	13.0	15.7	16.9
1979–81	13.3	14.3	17.1	18.6
1991	13.4	14.3	17.2	19.2
1998	14.3	16.1	17.4	19.3

Source: National Center for Health Statistics, Public Health Service, *Vital Statistics of the United States, 1992,* vol. 2: *Mortality* (Washington: Government Printing Office, 1996), section 6, table A. Figures for 1998 from Sherry L. Murphy, *Deaths: Final Data for 1998,* National Vital Statistics Reports, vol. 48, no. 11 (Hyattsville, Md.: National Center for Health Statistics, 2000), table 5.

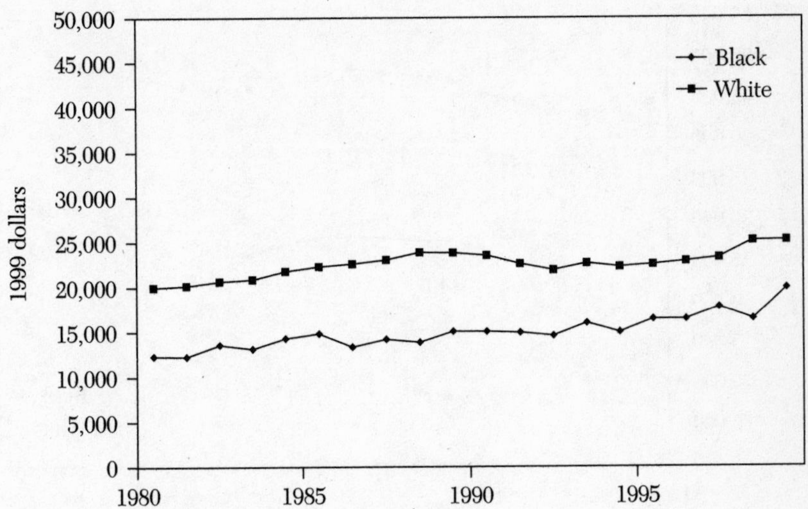

Figure 1. Median income, nonfamily households.
Source: U.S. Census Bureau, *Historical Income Tables—Households,* tables H-9A, H-9B. <www.census.gov/income/histinc/h09a.prn> and <www.census.gov/income/histinc/h09b.prn>

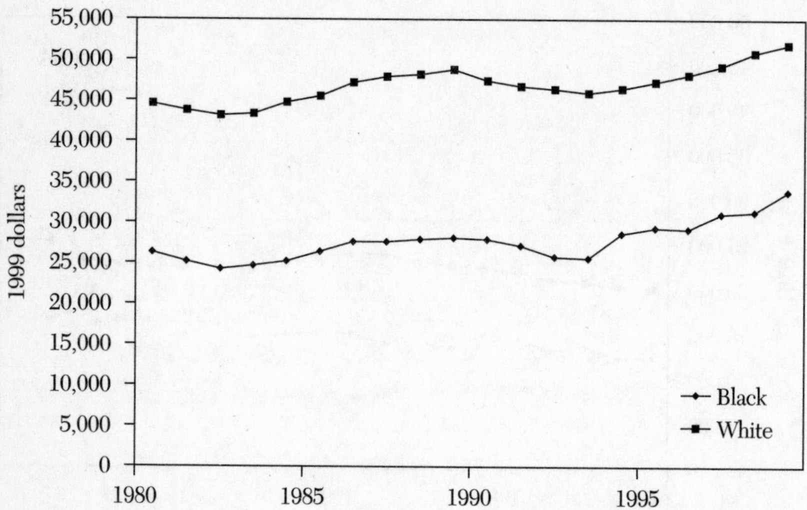

Figure 2. Median income, family households.
Source: U.S. Census Bureau, *Historical Income Tables—Households,* tables H-9A, H-9B. <www.census.gov/income/histinc/h09a.prn> and <www.census.gov/income/histinc/h09b.prn>

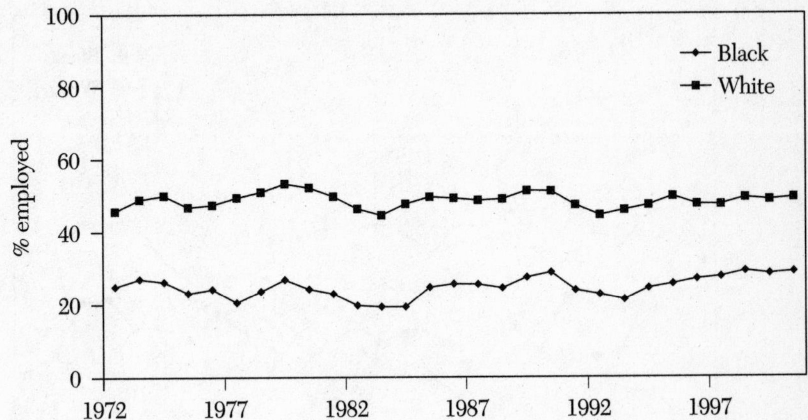

Figure 3. Employment-to-population ratio, ages 16–19.
Source: Bureau of Labor Statistics, *Labor Force Statistics from the Current Population Survey,* table A.2. <stats.bls.gov/webapps/legacy/cpsatab2.htm>

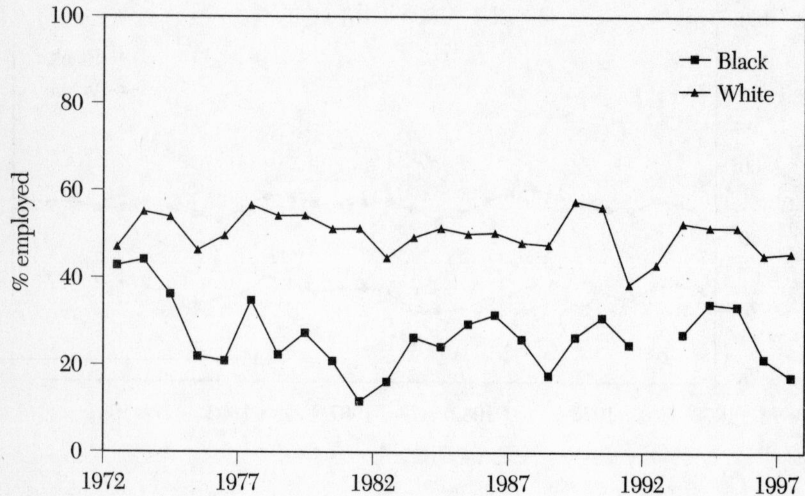

Figure 4. Employment of recent high school dropouts.
Source: National Center for Education Statistics, *Condition of Education, 1999*, supplemental table 10-4. <nces.ed.gov/pubs99/condition99/SupTables/supp-table-10-4.html>

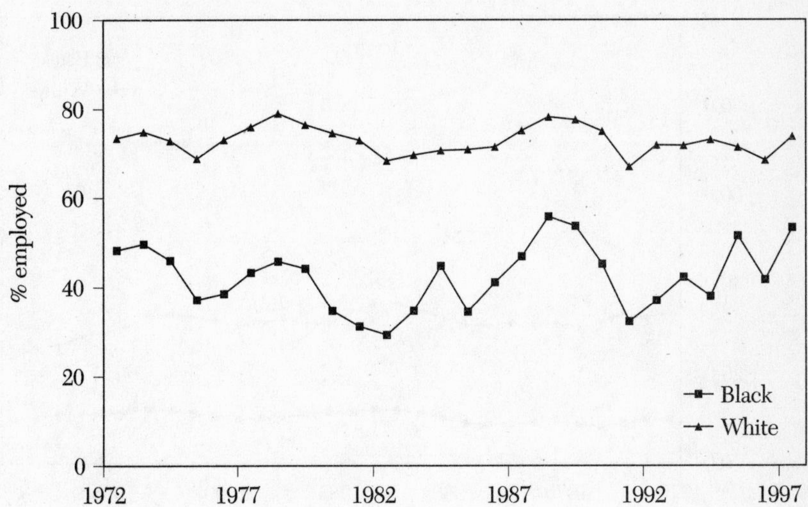

Figure 5. Employment of recent high school graduates.
Source: National Center for Education Statistics, *Condition of Education, 1999,* supplemental table 10-4. <nces.ed.gov/pubs99/condition99/SupTables/supp-table-10-4.html>

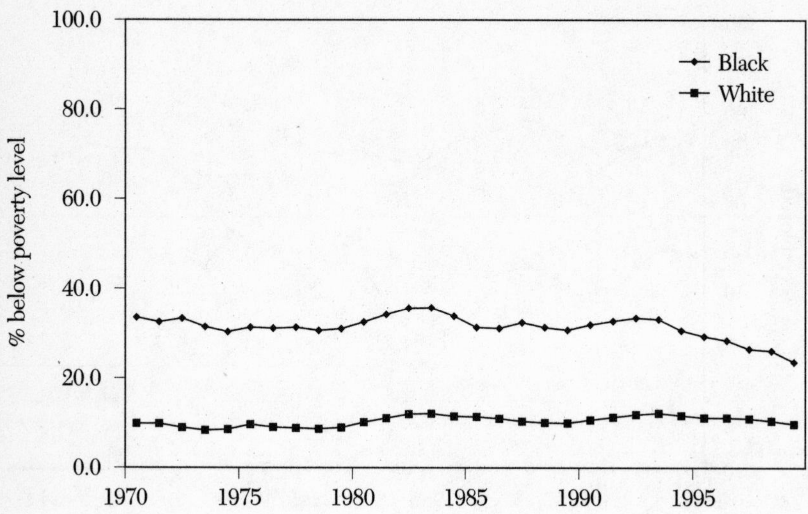

Figure 6. Poverty status of persons.
Source: Joseph Dalaker and Bernadette D. Proctor, *Poverty in the United States: 1999,* U.S. Census Bureau, Current Population Reports, Series P60-210 (Washington, 2000), table B.1.

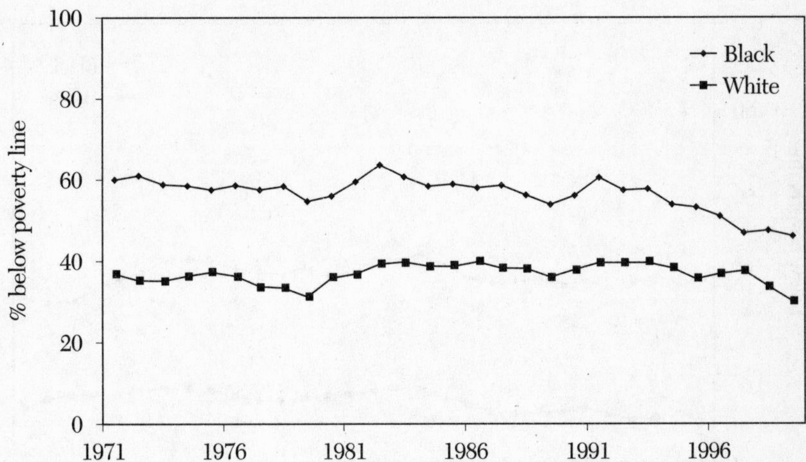

Figure 7. Poverty status of female-headed families (with children under 18).
Source: Joseph Dalaker and Bernadette D. Proctor, *Poverty in the United States: 1999,* U.S. Census Bureau, Current Population Reports, Series P60-210 (Washington, 2000), table B.3.

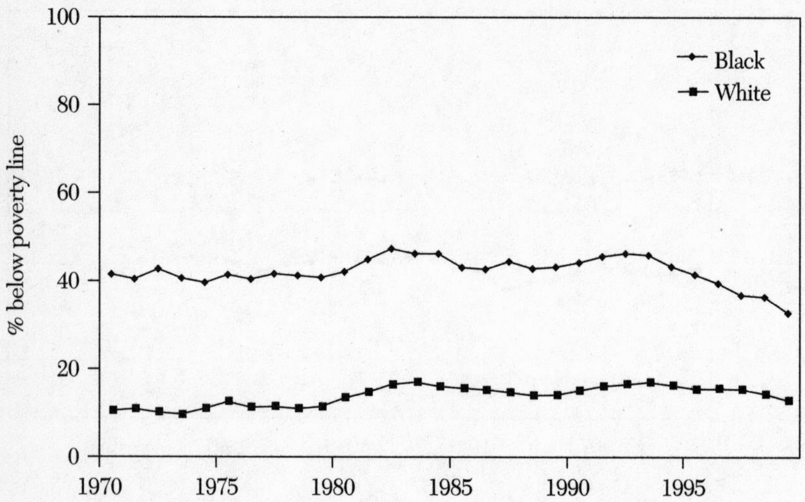

Figure 8. Poverty status of children under 18.
Source: Joseph Dalaker and Bernadette D. Proctor, *Poverty in the United States: 1999,* U.S. Census Bureau, Current Population Reports, Series P60-210 (Washington, 2000), table B.2.

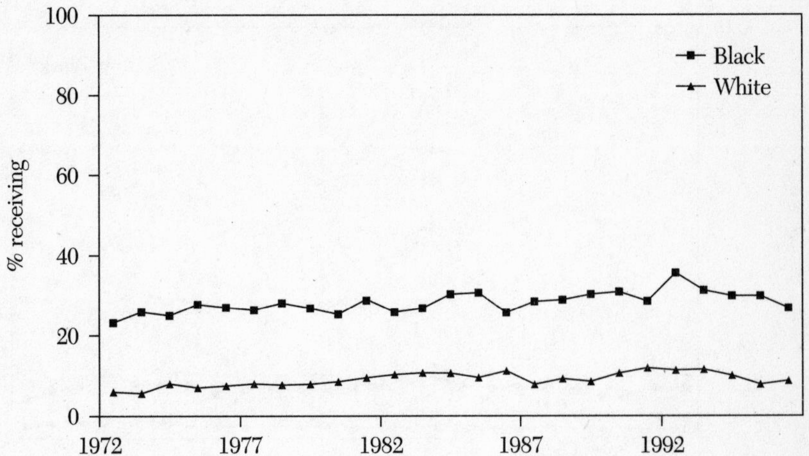

Figure 9. Receipt of AFDC or public assistance (ages 25–34 with 9–11 years of education).
Source: National Center for Education Statistics, *Condition of Education, 1998*, supplemental table 34-2. <nces.ed.gov/pubs98/condition98/c9834d02.html>

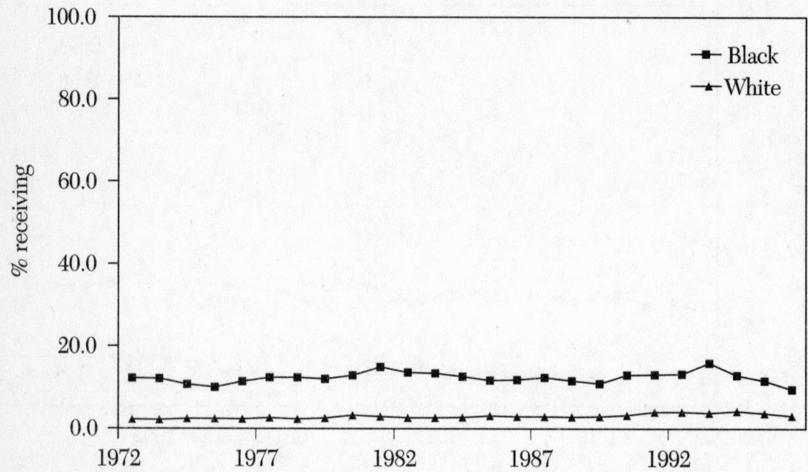

Figure 10. Receipt of AFDC or public assistance (ages 25–34 with 12 years of education).
Source: National Center for Education Statistics, *Condition of Education, 1998*, supplemental table 34-2. <nces.ed.gov/pubs98/condition98/c9834d02.html>

APPENDIX

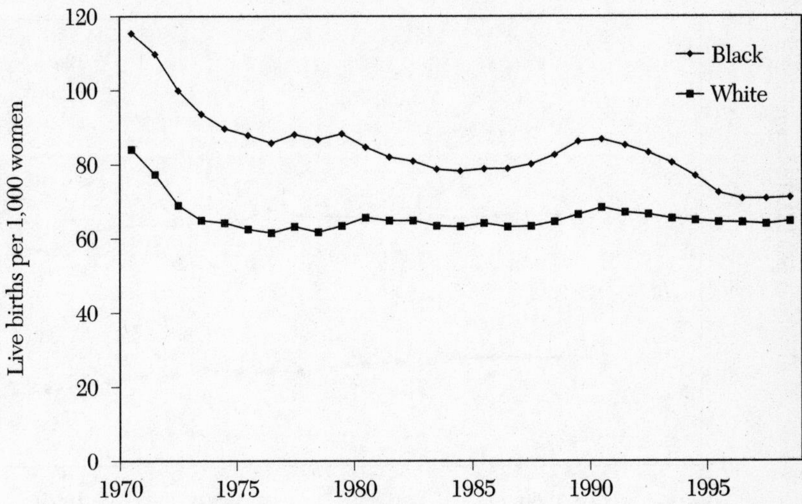

Figure 11. Birth rates, women aged 15–44.
Source: Stephanie J. Ventura, Joyce A. Martin, Sally C. Curtin, T. J. Mathews, and Melissa M. Park, *Births: Final Data for 1998,* National Vital Statistics Reports, vol. 48, no. 3 (Hyattsville, Md.: National Center for Health Statistics, 2000), table 1.

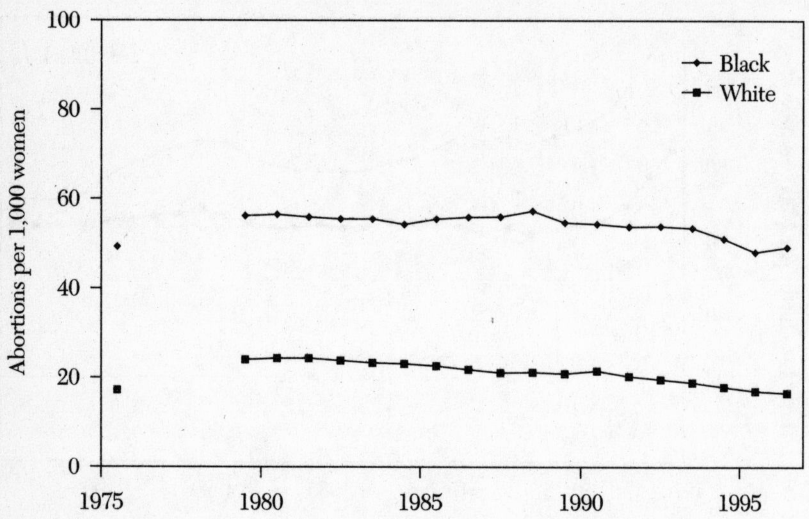

Figure 12. Abortions, women aged 15–44.
Source: U.S. Census Bureau, *Statistical Abstract of the United States: 1999* (Washington, 1999), table 123.

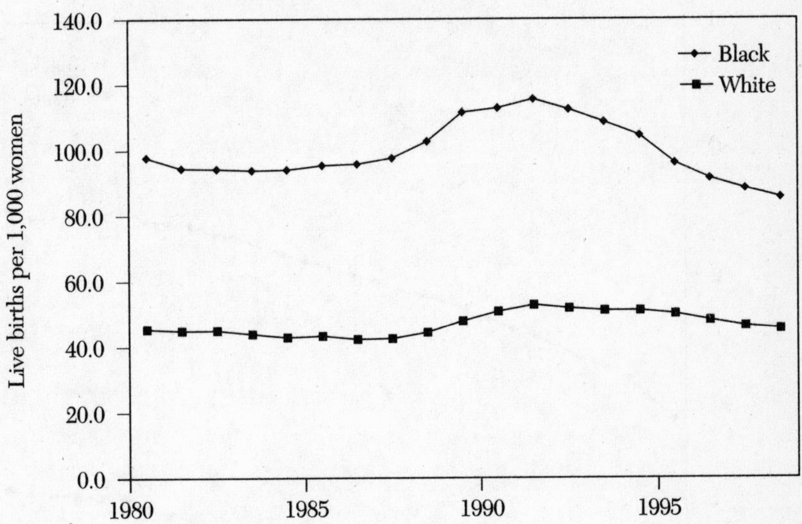

Figure 13. Birth rates, women aged 15–19.
Source: Stephanie J. Ventura, Joyce A. Martin, Sally C. Curtin, T. J. Mathews, and Melissa M. Park, *Births: Final Data for 1998,* National Vital Statistics Reports, vol. 48, no. 3 (Hyattsville, Md.: National Center for Health Statistics, 2000), table 4.

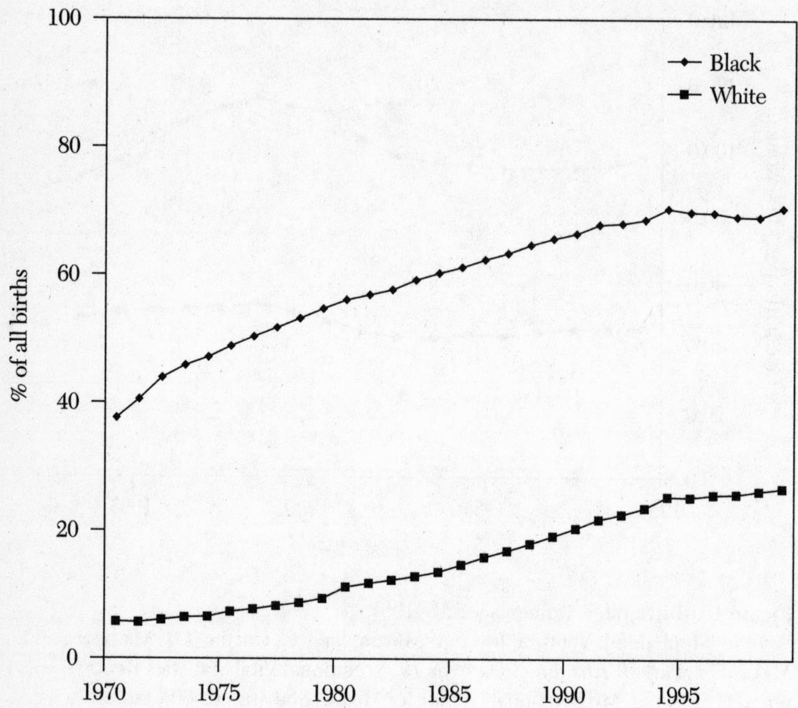

Figure 14. Births to unmarried mothers.
Source: Stephanie J. Ventura and Christine A. Bachrach, *Nonmarital Childbearing in the United States, 1940–99,* National Vital Statistics Reports, vol. 48, no. 16 (Hyattsville, Md.: National Center for Health Statistics, 2000), table 4.

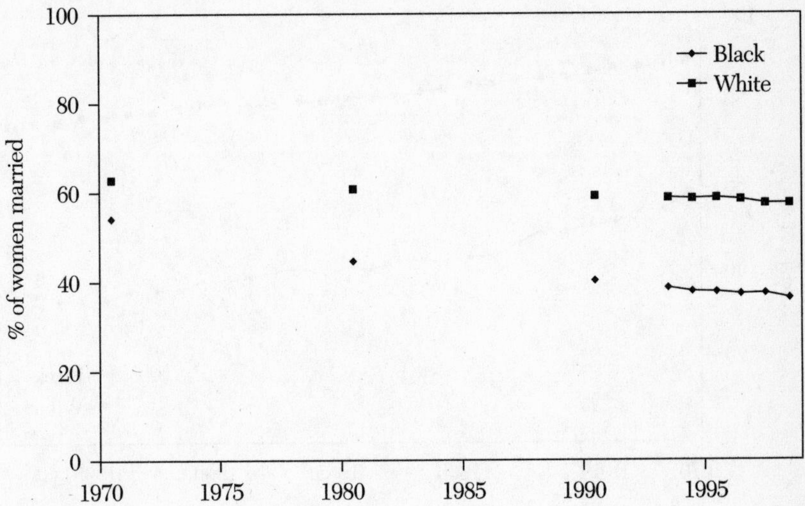

Figure 15. Percentage of women who are married, age 15 or older.
Source: U.S. Census Bureau, *Marital Status and Living Arrangements,* Historical Time Series, table MS-1 (Internet release date: January 7, 1999). <www.census.gov/population/socdemo/ms-la/tabms-1.txt>

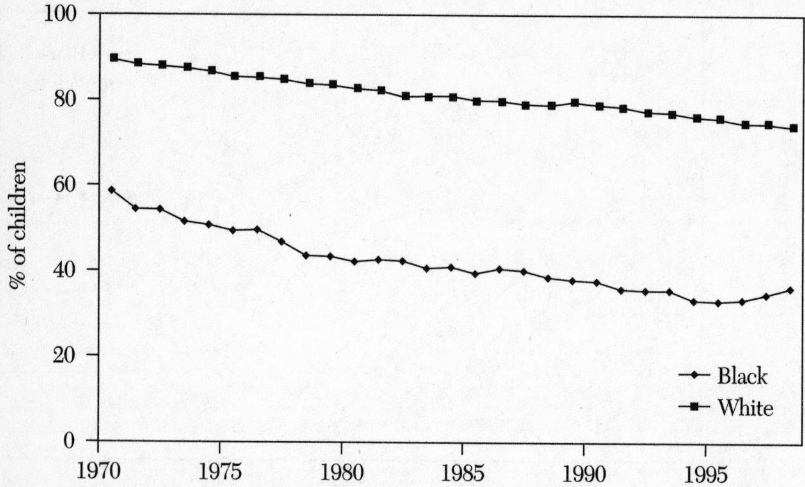

Figure 16. Children under age 18 living with both parents.
Source: U.S. Census Bureau, *Marital Status and Living Arrangements,* Historical Time Series, tables ch.2, ch.3 (Internet release date: January 7, 1999). <www.census.gov/population/socdemo/ms-la/tabch-2.txt> and <www.census.gov/population/socdemo/ms-la/tabch-3.txt>

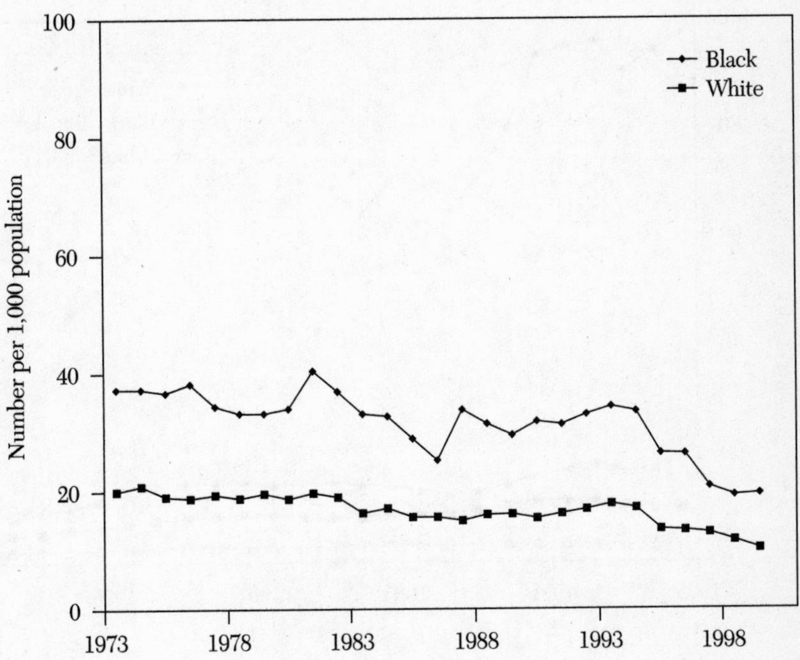

Figure 17. Victimization: Homicide, rapes, robberies, assaults (age 12 and older). *Source:* Bureau of Justice Statistics. <www.ojp.usdoj.gov/bjs/glance/race.txt>

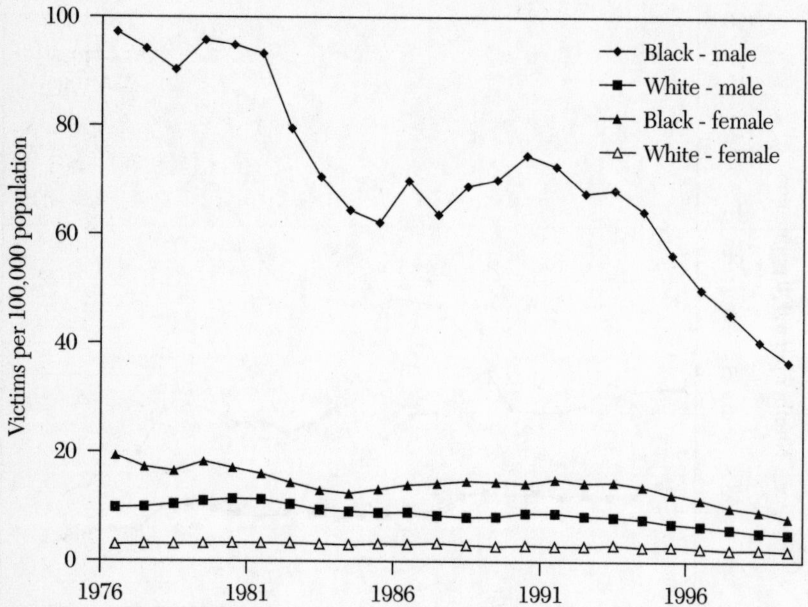

Figure 18. Victimization: Homicide (age 25 and older).
Source: James Alan Fox and Marianne W. Zawitz, *Homicide Trends in the United States,* U.S. Department of Justice, Bureau of Justice Statistics. <www.ojp.usdoj.gov/bjs/homicide/tables/varstab.htm>

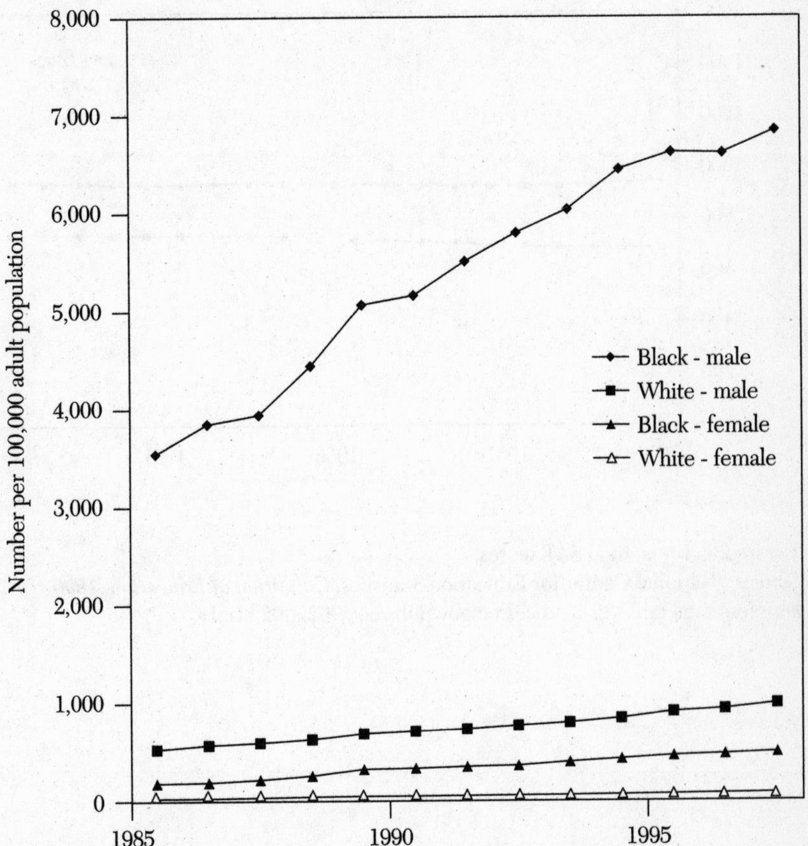

Figure 19. Adults held in local jails and state and federal prisons.
Source: Figures from 1985–1989: Bureau of Justice Statistics, *Correctional Populations in the United States, 1994* (Washington, 1996), NCJ 160091, table 1.7. Figures from 1990–1997: Bureau of Justice Statistics, *Correctional Populations in the United States, 1997* (Washington, 2000), NCJ 177613, table 1.7.

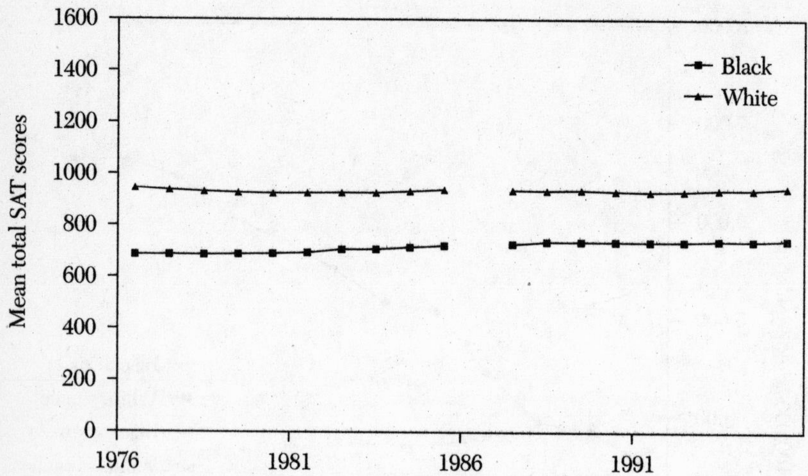

Figure 20. Mean total SAT scores.
Source: National Center for Education Statistics, *Condition of Education, 1996,* supplemental table 22-2. <nces.ed.gov/pubs/ce/c9622d02.html>

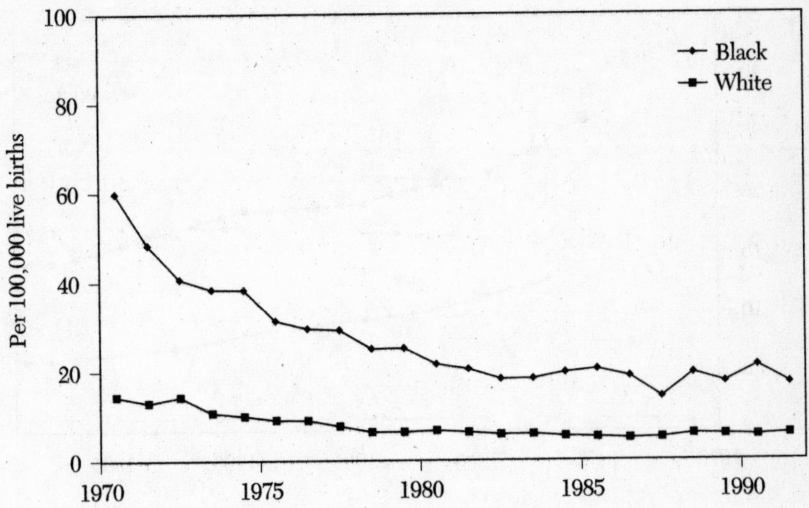

Figure 21. Maternal mortality.
Source: National Center for Health Statistics, *Vital Statistics of the United States, 1992*, vol. 2: *Mortality* (Washington, 1996).

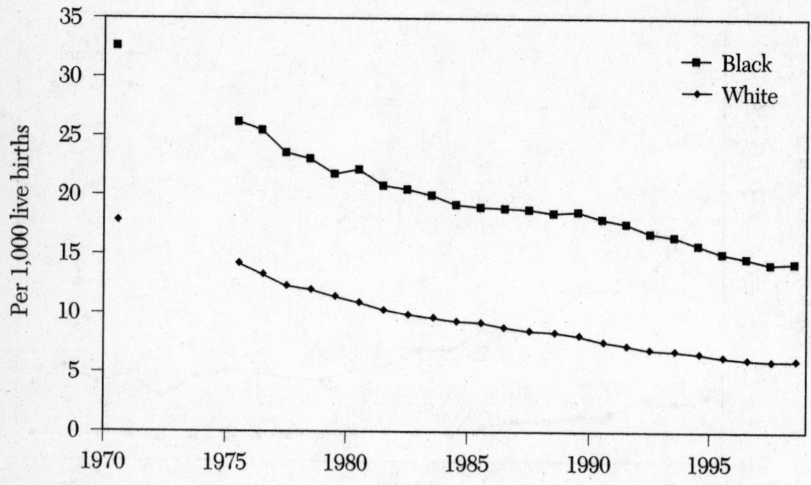

Figure 22. Infant mortality.
Source: Sherry L. Murphy, *Deaths: Final Data for 1998,* National Vital Statistics Reports, vol. 48, no. 11 (Hyattsville, Md.: National Center for Health Statistics, 2000), table 27.

NOTES

1. INTRODUCTION

1. I define "race" more precisely in Chapter 2. Until then, I use those quotation marks to caution the reader that the concept is fraught with scientific and ethical difficulties, and that I have in mind a rather specific and perhaps not universally accepted meaning when I invoke the term.
2. Since this book deals strictly with U.S. society, I use the terms "blacks" and "African Americans" interchangeably throughout, with no risk of ambiguity.
3. The reader may peruse the Appendix to see some statistical documentation of these claims.
4. I have long thought that applying Goffman's insights could illuminate the economic study of racial inequality, though I am aware of no serious attempt in this vein.
5. D'Souza 1995 is an especially stark example of this style of argument.
6. It might be objected at this point that even among native-born African Americans there are further distinctions to be drawn—between the children of recent Caribbean or African immigrants and those whose ancestors have been in the United States for many generations; or between those descended mainly from slaves and those whose ancestors were mainly "free persons of color." (Thomas Sowell makes much

of these very distinctions when discussing blacks; Sowell 1981.) But this observation, correct in principle, is of limited relevance to my purposes here. Thus Sowell's main point in drawing these intra-African-American contrasts is to argue that anti-black discrimination in the larger society takes us only so far when looking for an explanation of the social disadvantage of many blacks. As will become clear, I fully agree with this point. Nor do I presuppose that some monolithic, univalent, adverse perception of blacks by whites is the principal factor accounting for racial inequality.

2. RACIAL STEREOTYPES

1. Indeed, recent research in neuroscience suggests that perception of racial difference is deeply rooted in the human brain. Teams of brain scanners and social psychologists working in concert have recently found that a "particular part of the brain becomes more active when people look at members of a different race" (Berreby 2000, p. F3).
2. The phrase "racial classification" is also a term of art in the legal literature—with the Supreme Court pronouncing often on the conditions under which the use of racial classifications by governmental agents can be found consistent with the equal protection requirement of the Fourteenth Amendment. I will have essentially nothing to say here about that important but somewhat technical point of constitutional law.
3. I belabor this point because, in the partisan climate created by political struggle over race-based social policies, some commentators have taken to arguing that we ought to simply move beyond the discredited practice of "counting by race." In my opinion, an inquiry into the ethics of racial classification that never gets beyond the categorizing acts of individuals, so as to inquire into the virtue of the purposes on behalf of which those acts are being undertaken, is a rhetorical exercise that ought not to be taken seriously.
4. My definition is quite similar to that advanced by Stephen Cornell and Douglas Hartmann. They write: "A race is a group of human beings socially defined on the basis of physical characteristics. Determining

which characteristics constitute the race—the selection of markers and therefore the construction of the racial category itself—is a choice human beings make. Neither markers nor categories are predetermined by any biological factors. These processes of selection and construction are seldom the work of a moment. Racial categories are historical products and are often contested" (Cornell and Hartmann 1998, p. 24). With this definition in hand, I henceforth drop the fashionable practice of putting the word "race" in quotes, relying on the reader's understanding of what I intend with the term.

5. Eloquent and powerful arguments exposing ethical and philosophical problems with the "race" concept can be found in Gilroy 2000 and Appiah 1992. For a discussion of the scientific limitations of the "race" idea see Cavalli-Sforza 2000.

6. I will on occasion use "raced" as an adjective. Though this may strike the reader as odd, it is natural in the context of my argument. I simply want to be able to express with economy the notion that a person's fate is affected by racial categorization, or that the operation of a significant social institution is influenced by the practice of racial classification.

7. Again, I belabor what may be obvious only because the literature on the ethics of racial identification (self-classification) can be muddled on this point. For instance, Randall Kennedy argues that race-based feelings of loyalty, pride, and kinship are *ipso facto* morally problematic (Kennedy 1997). That argument is mistaken in my view, or, at best, it is woefully incomplete. It is not a moral error for a person subject to acts of racial classification, however ungrounded in objective taxonomy those acts may be, to take on as an operational and a psychological response some awareness of race that may serve to guide that agent's interrelations with others. An inquiry into the ethics of racial identification, racial loyalty, racial kinship, and racial attachment that never gets beneath the act of a single individual so identifying and so feeling, that never inquires into the structure within which that identifying, loyalty-feeling, kinship-affecting agent operates, ought not, in my humble opinion, to be taken seriously.

8. The economist A. Michael Spence was among the first to make this point. See Spence 1974.

9. Raising employers' review standards could also elicit greater effort from workers. But since an impossibly difficult standard makes effort superfluous, a tougher standard must discourage effort after some point. I am implicitly assuming in this thought experiment that by withholding the benefit of the doubt from black workers employers move beyond that point.
10. Bear in mind that this example is a thought experiment, and is not intended to be an explanation of today's crime statistics!
11. More generally, both types of young men could be discouraged by the drivers' reluctance to stop. What is required for this example to work is that *the proportion of robbers among those hailing cabs rises as the frequency of stops declines.* This condition will hold if the law abiding are more sensitive to delay than are those bent on robbery, which is quite plausible.
12. Of course some black buyers may be driven from the market altogether by this dealer behavior. But, as in the taxi example, when opting out is selective—with the toughest black bargainers being the first to withdraw, as seems plausible—the result will be to reinforce the dealers' stereotypic view of blacks as easy marks.
13. As with the workplace example, a tougher admissions standard could either encourage or discourage effort. Notice, however, that effort is superfluous if the standard is trivially easy or impossibly difficult to meet. Lowering the standard therefore discourages effort when one starts from a point where the standard is not too difficult, which is assumed to be the case here.
14. Another scenario could envision race-preferential admissions policies as having been objectively necessary at the start, but as creating self-confirming incentives that perpetuate reliance on these policies long after they have ceased to be objectively required. In any case, I want again to emphasize that these thought experiments are being offered here to illustrate the logic (and relevance) of my theory of stereotypes, and not to explain (or to criticize!) today's college admissions policies.
15. Regardless of which account he credits, in the real world of American society, beyond the confines of my thought experiments, a monopolistic observer has another important option: He can simply avail himself of an alternative source of labor exhibiting none of the problems asso-

ciated with blacks—by moving his operations to a different region, or hiring immigrant workers rather than African Americans. The interesting point here is that *negative stereotypes about one group may persist precisely because of the existence of positive stereotypes about another group* and vice versa. The two sets of beliefs can be mutually supportive via interacting, self-confirming feedback processes of the sort illustrated here. Although I cannot pursue this complication in this book, the questions it raises are of theoretical interest and, I think, also of practical importance. I am very much indebted to the sociologist John David Skrentny of the University of California at San Diego for comments that stimulated me to think in this direction.

16. The social psychology literature abounds with evidence supporting this claim. See the still useful though somewhat dated survey by Nisbett and Ross (1980).
17. The Yale University economist Hanming Fang has nicely formalized this insight. See Fang 1998.
18. The writer Brent Staples reported that he employed precisely this technique to avoid being reacted to as though he were a criminal while walking the streets of Chicago's Hyde Park neighborhood in the 1970s (Staples 1994).

3. RACIAL STIGMA

1. "Natal alienation" here refers to the circumstance in which slaves do not enjoy unfettered relations with their forebears, offspring, or mates. Rather, these are relations over which masters exert ultimate control.
2. See Skrentny 1996 for an illuminating exploration of how the development of race-preferential policies has been shaped by social meanings attached to race.
3. This point is further illustrated by a recent debate among N.F.L. officials over a proposed ban on players wearing bandannas and stocking caps under their helmets during games. According to the *New York Times* (George 2001), Dennis Green, the (black) head coach of the Minnesota Vikings, argued in favor of the ban during a closed meeting of owners and coaches in the spring of 2001: "Green, who has not

allowed Vikings players to wear bandannas or stocking caps in his 10 years in Minnesota, gave a speech about image, how he would not let his own child wear them and asked the group would they allow their children to wear them. He asked what the value in them was. If the image they projected is O.K., he asked, why do only a few of the league's hundreds of black players wear them? Would they allow their daughters to date a man with a bandanna?"

Green's position carried the day, with the owners voting 30–1 in favor of the ban (an exception was allowed for the skullcaps worn by some players to protect their scalps from abrasion). By way of explanation for the owners' decision, the *Times* observed: "Bandannas and stocking caps are linked to the hip-hop rap culture and also to gangs. They are, too, simply a fashion statement for some. But when you have been where the N.F.L. has been recently—murder trials, rape trials and boorish player behavior—the league showed its concern by passing stringent sportsmanship rules at the meetings. Clean it up. From head to toe." It is obvious that N.F.L. officials, black and white alike, are aware of the dire consequences for their financial interests that would ensue if the game's image were besmirched by the taint of racial stigma.

4. These differentially evolving speech patterns have been studied extensively by the sociolinguist William Labov of the University of Pennsylvania.

5. Of course, the adoption issue is complicated by the fact that many blacks oppose interracial adoptions (and interracial marriages, for that matter). Nor should an individual's decision (to adopt in Beijing rather than Baltimore, say) be taken as an accurate measure of that person's racial sympathies. It is likely that some prefer adopting Asian over African-American babies because, given their understanding of the social meaning of race in our culture, the prospect of raising an Asian child through a turbulent adolescence is less daunting than is the same prospect with a black child. However, it is also likely that some adoptive parents feel "safer" with a child not born in the ghetto because of the stigma-driven concern that, despite effective medical screening, an inner-city child may be defective in some way. In any event, I want again to acknowledge that the problems of biased cognition go in both directions—blacks (social workers adamantly opposed

to interracial adoption) can misperceive whites (prospective adopting parents). I would, however, venture the generalization that the consequences of biased social cognition for the achievement of a just public order are greatest when those with a distorted or incomplete vision of social reality, whatever may be their race, also control powerful levers of institutional discretion.

6. Documentation of the "hyper-segregation" of blacks in older American cities can be found in Massey and Denton 1993.
7. This story has been brilliantly told in the case of one American city by the University of Pennsylvania historian Thomas Sugrue. See Sugrue 1996.
8. Note that, whereas reward bias is purely an external matter (how disadvantaged persons are rewarded by outsiders for their expressed productivity), development bias may have both internal (to the group) and external sources. I will return to this point in Chapter 5.
9. Tilly 1998 captures precisely what I have in mind when calling attention to discrimination in contact. His parallel concept, "categorical inequality," is described as follows: "Durable inequality among categories arises because people who control access to value-producing resources solve pressing organizational problems by means of categorical distinctions. Inadvertently or otherwise, those people set up systems of social closure, exclusion, and control. Multiple parties—not all of them powerful, some of them even victims of exploitation—then acquire stakes in those solutions . . . Through all of these variations, we discover and rediscover paired, recognized, organized, unequal categories such as black/white, male/female, married/unmarried, and citizen/noncitizen" (pp. 7–8).

4. RACIAL JUSTICE

1. See Mills 1997, a provocative but in my view ultimately unpersuasive book.
2. My argument here is influenced by the work of James Fishkin. In Fishkin 1983 he defines a "tri-lemma" for liberalism, insofar as it is committed at one and the same time to the ideals of equality of opportunity, reward according to merit, and autonomy of the family. He

observes that autonomous but differentially endowed families will pass along differential developmental advantages to their children, some of whom, because rewards are distributed in reference to merit alone, will have superior life chances they have not earned, thus defeating the goal of achieving equal opportunity. A difficult choice, he concludes, must be made among these ideals.

3. This critique of liberalism is similar in spirit to the so-called communitarian arguments found in the work of Michael J. Sandel (1982) and Charles Taylor (1992), among others.
4. Thomas Sowell is perhaps the leading exponent of this view. See Sowell 1983.
5. Nozick 1974 provides a prototype of the procedural approach. I hasten to note that Nozick is himself aware of these difficulties. His "entitlement theory" of justice (ch. 7) consists of three parts: (1) an account of the just acquisition of holdings; (2) a theory of the just transfer of holdings; and (3) a principle of rectification which specifies how violations of requirements derived from (1) and (2) are to be handled. Thus Nozick's full system, if it could be implemented (he offers only a sketch of a theory), would not be incomplete in the sense being criticized here.
6. The argument of this section draws on Loury 1998.
7. See Tonry 1995 for an extended critique of U.S. drug policy along precisely these lines, and for compelling evidence in support of the claim that U.S. drug policy has led to young blacks being imprisoned disproportionately.
8. Obviously, there are also benefits to blacks from enforcement of anti-drug laws. This illustration is by no means intended to suggest that those benefits are slight. Taking them into account, and calculating the net impact of the policy on blacks as a group, would be entirely consistent with the spirit of the argument here.
9. Connerly 2000 provides an extended exposition of his views.
10. Some readers may object to my use here of the phrase "even some blacks." A critic's race is surely irrelevant, and my mention of it amounts to an *ad hominem* attack, one might hold. I think this objection is unfounded, and it may be useful to say why: If a critic's race is

used (even implicitly) to give authority to his or her argument, then he or she can hardly demand a race-blind evaluation of that argument. It is a fact about public life in the United States that the meaning of utterances—the sincerity or profundity of them—can depend on a speaker's race. A black adherent of race-blind liberalism, for instance, by publicly dissenting from a position most blacks endorse, does more than state an opinion. He or she will be understood as having taken a principled stand, *contra* filial attachment. This posture, more so than its content, may be what gives the criticism its public currency. Ironically, black advocates of race-blindness are busy denying the relevance of race, even as their race helps to make their denials relevant. This observation does not refute their arguments, nor does it prove them guilty of "racial disloyalty." But surely it is fair to take note of the irony.

11. Moskos and Butler 1996 documents this rationale for racial affirmative action in the U.S. Army.

12. *Hopwood v. Texas*, 1996, 78 F.3d 932.

REFERENCES

Anderson, Elijah. 1990. *Streetwise: Race, Class, and Change in an Urban Community.* Chicago: University of Chicago Press.

Appiah, Kwame Anthony. 1992. *In My Father's House: Africa in the Philosophy of Culture.* Oxford: Oxford University Press.

Arrow, Kenneth J. 1963. *Social Choice and Individual Values.* New Haven: Yale University Press.

Barnes, Barry. 1995. *The Elements of Social Theory.* Princeton: Princeton University Press.

Berreby, David. 2000. "How, but Not Why, the Brain Distinguishes Race." *New York Times,* September 5, p. F3.

Bourdieu, Pierre, and Loic J. D. Wacquant. 1992. *An Invitation to Reflexive Sociology.* Chicago: University of Chicago Press.

Bowen, William G., and Derek Bok. 1998. *The Shape of the River: Long-Term Consequences of Considering Race in College and University Admissions.* Princeton: Princeton University Press.

Cavalli-Sforza, Luigi L. 2000. *Genes, Peoples and Languages.* New York: North Point Press.

Charles, Camille Zubrinsky. 2000. "Neighborhood Racial-Composition Preferences: Evidenced from a Multiethnic Metropolis." *Social Problems,* 47, no. 3, pp. 379–407.

Coate, Stephen, and Glenn C. Loury. 1993a. "Antidiscrimination Enforcement and the Problem of Patronization." *American Economic Review,* 83, no. 2 (May), pp. 92–98.

——— 1993b. "Will Affirmative-Action Policies Eliminate Negative Stereotypes?" *American Economic Review,* 83, no. 5 (December), pp. 1220–40.

Connerly, Ward. 2000. *Creating Equal: My Fight against Race Preferences.* San Francisco: Encounter Books.

Cornell, Stephen, and Douglas Hartmann. 1998. *Ethnicity and Race: Making Identities in a Changing World.* Thousand Oaks, Calif.: Pine Forge Press.

D'Souza, Dinesh. 1995. *The End of Racism: Principles for a Multiracial Society.* New York: Free Press.

Fang, Hanming. 1998. "Discrimination with Endogenous Group Choices." Manuscript, Department of Economics, Yale University.

Farley, Reynolds. 1996. *The New American Reality: Who We Are, How We Got Here, Where We Are Going.* New York: Russell Sage Foundation.

Fishkin, James S. 1983. *Justice, Equal Opportunity, and the Family.* New Haven: Yale University Press.

Frazier, E. Franklin. 1957. *Black Bourgeoisie.* New York: Collier Books.

Freeman, Mike. 2000. "N.F.L. Hands Ravens' Lewis a Fine of $250,000, but Does Not Suspend Him." *New York Times,* August 18, p. D8.

George, Thomas. 2001. "Blacks at Center Stage in Debate on Headgear." *New York Times,* April 4, p. C21.

Gilens, Martin. 1999. *Why Americans Hate Welfare: Race, Media, and the Politics of Antipoverty Policy.* Chicago: University of Chicago Press.

Gilroy, Paul. 2000. *Against Race: Imagining Political Culture beyond the Color Line.* Cambridge, Mass.: Harvard University Press.

Goffman, Erving. 1959. *The Presentation of Self in Everyday Life.* New York: Doubleday.

——— 1963. *Stigma: Notes on the Management of Spoiled Identity.* New York: Simon and Schuster.

Herrnstein, Richard J., and Charles Murray. 1994. *The Bell Curve: Intelligence and Class Structure in American Life.* New York: Free Press.

Kennedy, Randall. 1997. "My Race Problem and Ours." *Atlantic Monthly,* May, pp. 55–66.

Kuhn, Thomas S. 1962. *The Structure of Scientific Revolutions.* Chicago: University of Chicago Press.

Loury, Glenn C. 1976. "Essays in the Theory of the Distribution of Income." Ph.D. thesis, Massachusetts Institute of Technology.

——— 1977. "A Dynamic Theory of Racial Income Differences." In *Women, Minorities and Employment Discrimination,* ed. P. A. Wallace and A. Lamond. Lexington, Mass.: Lexington Books.

——— 1995. *One by One from the Inside Out: Essays and Reviews on Race and Responsibility in America.* New York: Free Press.

——— 1998. "Foreword." In William G. Bowen and Derek Bok, *The Shape of the River,* pp. xxi–xxx. Princeton: Princeton University Press.

Massey, Douglas S., and Nancy Denton. 1993. *American Apartheid: Segregation and the Making of the Underclass.* Cambridge, Mass.: Harvard University Press.

Mills, Charles W. 1997. *The Racial Contract.* Ithaca: Cornell University Press.

——— 1998. *Blackness Visible: Essays on Philosophy and Race.* Ithaca: Cornell University Press.

Moskos, Charles C., and John Sibley Butler. 1996. *All That We Can Be: Black Leadership and Racial Integration the Army Way.* New York: Basic Books.

Myrdal, Gunnar. 1944. *An American Dilemma: The Negro Problem and Modern Democracy.* New York: Pantheon.

Nisbett, Richard E., and Lee Ross. 1980. *Human Inference: Strategies and Shortcomings of Social Judgment.* Englewood Cliffs, N.J.: Prentice-Hall.

Nozick, Robert. 1974. *Anarchy, State and Utopia.* New York: Basic Books.

Patterson, Orlando. 1982. *Slavery and Social Death.* Cambridge, Mass.: Harvard University Press.

——— 1998. *Rituals of Blood: Consequences of Slavery in Two American Centuries.* Washington: Civitas.

Sandel, Michael J. 1982. *Liberalism and the Limits of Justice.* Cambridge: Cambridge University Press.

Skrentny, John D. 1996. *The Ironies of Affirmative Action: Politics, Culture, and Justice in America.* Chicago: University of Chicago Press.

Sniderman, Paul M., and Thomas Piazza. 1993. *The Scar of Race.* Cambridge, Mass.: Harvard University Press.

Soss, Joe, Sanford Schram, Thomas Vartanian, and Erin O'Brien. 2001. "Setting the Terms of Relief: Political Explanations for State Policy Choices in the Devolution Revolution." *American Journal of Political Science,* 45, no. 2 (April), pp. 378–395.

Sowell, Thomas. 1981. *Ethnic America: A History.* New York: Basic Books.

——— 1983. *The Economics and Politics of Race: An International Perspective.* New York: William Morrow.

Spence, A. Michael. 1974. *Market Signaling: Informational Transfer in Hiring and Related Screening Processes.* Cambridge, Mass.: Harvard University Press.

Staples, Brent A. 1994. *Parallel Time: Growing Up in Black and White.* New York: Pantheon.

Sugrue, Thomas J. 1996. *The Origins of the Urban Crisis: Race and Inequality in Postwar Detroit.* Princeton: Princeton University Press.

Taylor, Charles. 1992. *Multiculturalism and the Politics of Recognition.* Princeton: Princeton University Press.

Thernstrom, Stephan, and Abigail Thernstrom. 1997. *America in Black and White: One Nation, Indivisible.* New York: Simon and Schuster.

Tilly, Charles. 1998. *Durable Inequality.* Berkeley: University of California Press.

Tocqueville, Alexis de. 1848. *Democracy in America.* New York: Harper and Row.

Tonry, Michael. 1995. *Malign Neglect: Race, Crime, and Punishment in America.* New York: Oxford University Press.

Wacquant, Loic J. D. 1993. "Urban Outcasts: Stigma and Division in the Black American Ghetto and the French Urban Periphery." *International Journal of Urban and Regional Research,* 17, no. 3 (September), pp. 366–383.

Zinsmeister, Karl. 1996. "Painful but Productive: Toward Honesty on Race." *American Enterprise,* 7, no. 1 (January-February), pp. 4–6, 20.

INDEX

INDEX

INDEX

INDEX

INDEX